MANAGING
AND LEADING
NONPROFIT
ORGANIZATIONS

MANAGING

AND LEADING

NONPROFIT

ORGANIZATIONS

A Framework for Success

PAUL L. DANN

WILEY

Published by John Wiley & Sons, Inc., Hoboken, New Jersey.
Published simultaneously in Canada.

For general information on our other products and services or for technical support, please contact our Customer Care Department within the United States at (800) 762-2974, outside the United States at (317) 572-3993 or fax (317) 572-4002.

Wiley also publishes its books in a variety of electronic formats. Some content that appears in print may not be available in electronic formats. For more information about Wiley products, visit our web site at www.wiley.com.

Library of Congress Cataloging-in-Publication Data:

Names: Dann, Paul L., author.
Title: Managing and leading nonprofit organizations : a framework for
    success / Paul L. Dann.
Description: Hoboken, New Jersey : Wiley, [2022] | Includes bibliographical
    references and index.
Identifiers: LCCN 2021038148 (print) | LCCN 2021038149 (ebook) | ISBN
    9781119818533 (hardback) | ISBN 9781119818557 (adobe pdf) | ISBN
    9781119818540 (epub)
Subjects: LCSH: Nonprofit organizations—Management. | Leadership.
Classification: LCC HD62.6 .D365 2022 (print) | LCC HD62.6 (ebook) | DDC
    658/.048—dc23
LC record available at https://lccn.loc.gov/2021038148
LC ebook record available at https://lccn.loc.gov/2021038149

Cover image: © TortugaStudios/Shutterstock
Cover design: Wiley

SKY10030950_120221

For my wife, Patti, who always supports and believes in me.

Contents

1

Introduction and Purpose
of This Book

I REMEMBER MY first formal leadership assignment with great clarity. I had been working as a case manager serving delinquent youth placed in foster care. My executive director had called me quite out of the blue to ask if I might assist with a situation that had arisen within one of the organization's community residences for young people who were transitioning from the state psychiatric hospital back into the community. Apparently, the staff within the residence had "run off" the former program director. It was an uprising of the finest order, a vote of no confidence in his leadership such that the entire staff team was threatening to walk.

When I arrived on the site it was clear that I was not welcome. I still recall the steely greeting and the lack of willingness to engage with me, even at the most basic level. Somehow, I represented the administration and there was no way in hell that the team was going to allow me any opportunity to fill a leadership role. Over the next few months I had what could only be called a baptism by fire. As if in the pitch dark I worked carefully to feel my way through the challenges of becoming accepted as a leader by a disenchanted team. More than once I stumbled and found myself tripping over or even into one difficult situation after another. There were certainly lessons learned and each lesson came with its share of bumps and bruises. There were also breakthrough moments that were a combination of happenstance and strategy gone well.

In this instance, I was thrown into a leadership role with only my wits and whatever sensibility I possessed about the human condition and what it would take for people to once again trust someone in a leadership role. Since that time, now more than 40 years later, I have come across many opportunities to develop my leadership and management capacity. Some of these opportunities mirrored my first formal leadership assignment, necessitating that I knock around in the dark with an ever-emergent understanding of what needed to be done, a live-and-learn method. Other learning opportunities were more formal in nature, through training or education; some were supported by the colleagues and mentors I encountered within the field along the way; and still others came from the work itself. The people we serve, the team, and the experiences you have within the nonprofit field combine to teach you while you strive to make a difference in the world.

After four decades it's remarkable to consider what I have learned through this experience about nonprofit leadership and nonprofit management. There are many lessons learned, some of which demonstrate the simplest strategies to implement effective leadership and some that are by nature more complex, requiring more of one's attention as well as practice to master. And then there are the lessons that fall into the category that is simultaneously simple and complex, where the resulting leadership practice is straightforward yet filled with many layers of dynamism, purpose, and potential.

I must admit that leadership strategies that maintain a simultaneous stance of being simple and complex are among the most intriguing and, incidentally, when mastered, the most potent when it comes to advancing your nonprofit leadership capabilities. In accord with Jeffrey Kluger's (2008) work I have come to think about the presence of simultaneous simplicity and complexity within organizational leadership as *simplexity*. The idea of simplexity used this way can be considered the presence of simple strategies that have within them multiple layers as well as significant implication for leadership practice. This conceptual frame is similar in some ways to Koestler's classic idea of a holon, where something is simultaneously a part of something else while being whole in and of itself (1967). Of note in the conceptual frame of a holon is the importance of the interconnectivity between the two. Like a holon, strategies within simplexity can stand alone and at the same time are interdependent.

An illustrative way to think about the presence and use of simplexity and its potential for impact is to consider how country or blues music is structured. Country music is largely built using three chords with a chorus, blues music with three chords in a repetitive progression. Simple, right? Well, yes and no; if you consider each genre, it will not take you long to realize the depth and scope of the music that has resulted from these simple patterns. Furthermore, if you have ever picked up a guitar and tried to become the next Garth Brooks or B.B. King, you will quickly realize just how tough it is to take the basic chord patterns found in each genre and become the next music legend. Mastering strategies that engage simplexity takes time as well as specific tried-and-true strategies. Do not worry: this book will help you with this as well as other strategies to advance your leadership practice.

This book is an effort to capture the lessons learned from decades of effective nonprofit leadership practice. The goal is to help you avoid, if you wish, some of the knocking around in the dark that comes from being unsure about how to move forward with a leadership situation. And while no amount of teaching or sharing of strategies and techniques can make it possible to avoid instances of "baptism by fire," this book will assist you in developing a leadership toolbox that will help you advance as a nonprofit leader and manager.

The notion of a leadership toolbox is an important one. Leadership performed well requires that you develop a set of capabilities that can be drawn upon to help advance your goals and objectives. Each of these capabilities have their own nuances and require that you become skilled at implementing them. As we discuss in Chapter 2, being successful in leadership requires practice, similar to the way using a tool requires that you know its purpose and that you have worked enough

Build Your Leadership Toolbox!

with it to understand what it offers as well as its limitations, not to mention the level of skill that you bring to its use.

Many of us can recall a former leader or manager (you may have one at this very moment!) who knew how to use only one or two tools of what should have been a complete toolbox for leadership practice. The leader who has only a hammer is ill equipped for the complexity we find in today's organizations—not all problems are nails in need of a hammer. At the risk of over-using the metaphor, try hiring someone to build your house and see how it goes if they know only how to hammer things. It is not a pretty sight, and the desired goal will be destined to fail. It's comical when you think about a carpenter who can manage only the swing of a hammer, pounding away in an endless effort to cut a board or tighten a screw, only to fail in the end. We laugh at the image, but the truth is that many managers and leaders find themselves with only one or two tools that they have become relatively proficient with. Let's not stick to the same few tools and instead commit ourselves to building a proper set of tools to help advance your capabilities to effectively lead.

The goal of this book is to help you develop your leadership and managerial capabilities. The toolbox seen here contains tried-and-true tools. Like the toolbox metaphor, the idea behind this book is to share tried-and-true strategies that will assist you throughout your leadership practice within the nonprofit industry. By using tried-and-true strategies, you will be prepared to refine and develop your leadership toolbox.

Now it is true that some might criticize the use of tried-and-true tools as turning a blind eye to what is new and emerging. The intent here is not to exclude new and emergent strategies—in fact we will explore some of what is new and upcoming—but rather to impart what has been learned as successful strategies for advancing leadership over the course of four decades of successful nonprofit leadership.

This book also endeavors to help you heighten your capacity for what I call scholar/practice-based leadership. The book draws upon what is written about leadership practice in today's complex organizations and importantly delves into practice-based strategies and techniques. In this way we integrate what is known in the literature about best practices within nonprofit leadership while exploring practical strategies to ensure the efficacy of your leadership practice. It is important to know what works and how your practice is grounded in what is written about effective leadership as you strive to support the people you serve and the organizations you work for.

Together we work through the lessons learned with an eye toward supporting the development of your leadership practice. Chapter 2 identifies the importance of building your practice, not only for yourself but also for those around you. Contrary to the traditional Western Cultural lens, leadership is not a lone wolf activity where a single actor ensures a successful outcome but rather an activity that, when done well, requires processes that engage the skills of the individual, the entire team, and the overall organization.

In Chapter 3 we explore some key leadership models that you can use to identify your own leadership approach. This is a 1,000-foot flyover and could be a book in and of itself. The goal here, however, is to provide you with some sense of where your leadership practice either lives or will live as you grow into your leadership style and approach. You will also read about some classic conceptual frames for leadership that I have found to be extremely helpful. Like our box of tried-and-true leadership tools, many of the classic frames for leadership practice have true value as we develop our skills and capabilities.

In Chapter 4 we delve into strategies for impacting organizational culture. Here we encounter the conceptual frame of simplexity where many of the strategies are at once "simple and complex." As in the earlier chapters, Chapter 4 will provide you with an opportunity to enhance your leadership practice as well as the practice of those around you within the organization. The organization's culture is critical to the success of any nonprofit agency and so we give the importance of establishing a positive organizational culture its due in this chapter, returning to these important ideas as appropriate throughout the book.

Chapter 5 explores the practice of Generative Leadership, where leadership development is achieved through leadership in action. Generative Leadership provides you with a way to advance your own, your team's, and your organization's capacity to grow effective leadership. In many ways this becomes the secret sauce for you and your organization's continued success, so be ready to make use of the strategies that are imparted here.

In Chapter 6 we underscore the benefits that can come from engaging our most precious resource: our employees. Through performance management and employee engagement we unlock more of the strategies that have proven to be extraordinarily successful when working to advance leadership practice within and across the organization. Simplexity abounds here as well, particularly when you consider how simple yet critically important the ideas are for ensuring your team or organization's ability to achieve its nonprofit mission.

Chapter 7 explores the use of effective systems to realize desired outcomes for your organization. Thoughtful development and use of systems are critical to ensuring that you can achieve the goals and objectives identified as part and parcel of your organization's purpose, mission, and vision. As you read this chapter, you will see the importance of ensuring that you have built a dynamic and thoughtful set of systems that complement your structure and the values, beliefs, and vision that you hold essential to achieving the organization's mission.

I would be remiss if this book did not also explore the topic of change and the importance of establishing a leadership practice that has the capacity for change management. Chapter 8 does just that by discussing various strategies to ensure effective change management. In today's complex organizations, having a leadership practice that is equipped to manage and guide your team and organization through change is essential. We take time to ensure that the capacity for change management is multilayered by going beyond the prowess of the individual leader to change management at the team and the organizational level.

In addition, do not forget the importance of conflict management, which is explored in detail within Chapter 9. Conflict is a part of everyday organizational life and when it's managed well, it can become a source of growth and development for you, your team, and the entire organization.

In Chapter 10 I share some of the techniques and strategies I have used to engage and advance my team. Many of the strategies here are drawn from years of experience supervising and motivating team members to be their best. Your ability to lead effectively is directly connected to your capacity to develop a strong team. Given this, I think you will find this chapter quite helpful.

In Chapter 11 we explore the world of leadership that lives just outside the metes and bounds of your own organization by helping you to understand the nature of strategic alliances, how they can benefit you, and what opportunities they represent. It is important, as you develop your leadership capacity, to consider how your leadership practice engages with those who are outside the internal activities that typically draw attention and cry out for your focus. Knowing how to exercise your leadership practice with external stakeholders will provide you with new and interesting opportunities to help advance the work and mission of your organization.

Chapter 12 is an effort to bring it all together, knowing of course that each chapter in and of itself will become a resource for you. Within this context I recommend that you take time to read this book from cover to cover, yet also feel free to move between the chapters in a way that serves your current context and interest. In this way the book can become like a home-repair book. If you found one morning that your pipes had burst (Chapter 4 in our imaginary home-repair book), you would not start reading from Chapter 1, would you? With the water pouring down I am confident that you would jump straight to Chapter 4 and realize that step one is to cut off the water. Feel free to use this book in the same manner. For example, when I walked into my first leadership role, now more than 40 years ago, I would have turned to Chapters 4 and 6 before reading Chapter 1.

As you will see in the Appendix, I have also included several tools that relate to specific topic areas within the various chapters that you can use to assess your own, your team's, or your organization's leadership and management practice. Each tool is connected to what is explored in a specific chapter and as a result the tools can be used to support as well as advance the information in the related chapter. For example, the Employee Engagement and Performance Assessment tool can help you to operationalize what is discussed in Chapter 6, not only for yourself but also for your team. Each tool has been tried and tested in my own leadership practice and has played a role in advancing effective leadership practice at the individual, team, and organizational level. I think you will find that these tools serve you well as you work to move from theory to practice and implement the various strategies shared within this book.

2

Leadership as Practice

MALCOLM GLADWELL (2008) is credited with defining the amount of practice needed to master a desired skill. His observation that excellence in any endeavor requires 10,000 hours of practice is widely quoted and, while pundits argue about the veracity of the claim, we can agree that anything worth learning takes practice. While some people seem to have a natural ability for a given activity it is also true that people can be taught. This is true for leadership as well (Doh, 2003). Some people may have characteristics that support their ability to be an effective leader while others may find themselves with fewer innate abilities to support them at the onset. Despite these differences individuals have the capacity to build their leadership capability through thoughtful practice.

For example, I had a manager who was extremely introverted, and it pained her to speak with large groups. It literally took every bit of strength she had to talk within our group gatherings, never mind the stress that she experienced when presenting to a group at a formal conference. As a contrast, I had another manager who was quick-witted and extremely comfortable presenting to groups and seemed to become more energized as the group size grew. A true extrovert! Now, the introvert had much more technical knowledge and had spent a great amount of time studying and learning the content that was to be presented. In contrast our extrovert's ability to work the crowd created a dynamic where there was not much concern about knowing the content. As you can see, in either instance there is a great deal to learn. The introvert needed to work on her capacity to present publicly by building strategies to handle her discomfort while the extrovert needed to learn the importance of being fully prepared. Given this it is important for every leader to actively pursue their own leadership development no matter what capabilities they bring at the onset.

The notion of actively pursuing your own leadership development means, in a practical sense, that you commit yourself to a path of continual leadership development, a path that ensures you build on your existing strengths and areas for improvement in an ongoing way. Commit yourself to pursuing ongoing learning about leadership and take what you are learning to build your leadership practice. If you do not learn and then practice, you will cut short your own development and stunt your growth as a nonprofit leader.

Leadership development is like muscle development. If you do not work out, then you will not build muscle mass. Conversely if you commit to working out, then you will build muscle mass. As an illustration of this, if you have ever broken a bone and had a cast, you will be familiar with the surreal feeling you had as you looked at your arm the moment the cast was removed. The muscle on the recently healed arm is essentially gone and the first thought you have is "Whose arm is this?" The arm still belongs to the original owner, it is just that the lack of exercise and mobility has caused muscle atrophy. In a like manner if you do not regularly exercise your leadership skills, you will experience the loss of leadership muscle.

In addition to working to develop your own leadership muscle it is important to consider strategies to build leadership capability at the team as well as organizational level. In today's complex nonprofit organizations, we come to recognize the importance of expanding the entire organization's leadership prowess. No longer can we rely on the individual positional leader to carry the team and the organization forward. We are better served if the entire team has the ability to act in a leadership capacity.

So, in a very real sense it is important to commit to thinking about your own, your team's, and your organization's capacity for leadership as a *leadership practice* that is built on what is known to work well in order to support the goals, objective, vision, and mission of your organization. The master carpenter that successfully learns the use of her tools engages in the practice of carpentry. She has learned and refined the various skills pertaining to each tool and knows from the knowledge base that has been developed what to use and when to use them. Then by plying her trade each day she continually refines her skills and capabilities. Your plan should be to grow into this metaphor from a leadership perspective and ensure that you as well as your entire team and your overall organization work to continually build a leadership practice.

As we explore some of the specific tools that you will want to develop, it's important to consider several perspectives about leadership practice that I have found to be extremely helpful. Each of the practice perspectives explored in this chapter provides a lens to help you better understand your work as a leader.

First Practice Perspective: Being Antigravitational

My long-standing mentor often says that to be effective we must often be "antigravitational." The notion itself conjures up odd visions of people floating above the ground, but despite the humorous nature of the vision the conceptual frame is a useful one. To be gravitational is to simply go with the flow. To be *antigravitational* means that there are times when one should move against the flow, to work in a way that moves in the opposite direction of what would come naturally, to give pause to the pull that typically exists—at least long enough to understand what other options might exist.

Simply going with the gravitational pull means that you are acting without critical thought regarding the actions that you are undertaking. Being antigravitational means that you are taking stock in the current situation and that you have made a mindful decision to move against or away from the direction that is formed by the norms found within the cultural context. For example, growing up you may have received messages from your parents and the people around you that you should not create a problem: "Don't make a fuss," "It's not that big a deal," or "Mind your own business" could be a tape that plays over and over again in your head. The gravitational pull in this context would be to simply keep quiet and avoid raising any concern. This pull follows you into your work and into your leadership practice. To be antigravitational you would need to move against this gravitational pull and instead work to ensure that you speak up, that you work to address concerns as well as understand that getting involved *is* your business.

To be gravitational is to risk action without thought. To be antigravitational is to ensure that you have exercised a thoughtful examination of your and others' actions to determine whether a different course of action—one that is against the flow—is the better course of action. The key here in understanding this perspective is to understand the role that awareness and mindfulness plays in determining whether to be gravitational or antigravitational. The notion is not to always be a contrarian, but rather to ensure that your leadership practice includes the mindful consideration of your and your team's actions. Understand that there are times when you must go against the flow, and that in order to know when to do this you have to be aware of exactly what the flow is and where it comes from.

Second Practice Perspective: The Long View

Tomlinson (2007) underscores that we find ourselves in a culture of speed, where there is a continual move toward getting things done more quickly. Faster is better, getting it done is key, and arriving at the destination is held as paramount. The need for immediacy has become a driving force in our society. Consider how food is prepared, packaged, and ready to go, even mailed to you in portions that you can drop in a pot. Think about the desire for faster, more efficient forms of transportation and how impatient we have all become when we are ready for something. One only needs to look at the phenomenon of same-day delivery, books and movies on demand, and push-button solutions to see that our cultural desire for immediacy has become pervasive.

The impact of this culture of immediacy goes beyond the delivery of packages and the use of high-speed internet, extending as well into the very way in which we conduct ourselves professionally. We quickly become impatient and want the end rewards even before we have begun the journey.

Successful leadership requires a different perspective. We must be antigravitational and recognize that many things come over time. It is not possible to push a button or flick a switch to become effective as a leader. To develop as a leader and a strong manager you must practice, pursue learning opportunities, and avail yourself of leadership experiences—experiences that help to ensure both the presence of practice and learning opportunities.

In my work with aspiring leaders, I often find myself asking them the question "Where are you going?" I generally receive a puzzled look, to which I respond, "No, where are you going?" The question becomes a point of reflection. "Why are you in such a rush?" To stop and consider what one is doing and where one is going and the pace at which one is pursuing their journey is key. We rush, go, and do, but we rarely take a moment to consider what we are doing and why we are rushing.

Taking the long view requires that we acknowledge that our goals and objectives in leadership will take time—that there is little benefit to rushing and those who have a long view will have an advantage over those who feel they must already be at their destination. Consider the success of the marathon runner who understands that their effort requires a different strategy than that of the runner in the 100-yard dash. To have a long-view perspective is to be tenacious in your pursuit of leadership and managerial prowess. Do not give up and do not burn yourself out by setting unrealistic expectations about what it will take to advance your leadership practice.

Third Practice Perspective: It's the Journey, Not the Destination

Just as we need to learn to take the long view, we should strive to understand the role that the journey plays in your leadership development. Because we become obsessed with getting there and reaching the destination, we often forget the importance of the journey itself. Effective leaders understand that the journey they have embarked upon in the development of their practice represents simultaneously an opportunity to learn and grow as well as a source of enjoyment. Do not miss out on the ability to enjoy as well as revel in the path you have chosen to advance your growing leadership practice. One strategy to help ensure this is to work toward being present in your day-to-day work. Rather than being driven by the outcome or the goal take time to appreciate what you experience along the way.

I think, for example, about the amazing things I encounter in my own nonprofit leadership practice every day. For example, when the COVID-19 pandemic began, the six-month leadership academy that I offered for aspiring leaders was stalled and looked like it would be doomed for the next year. The goal of advancing our leaders seemed sidelined, until one of my team members suggested I simply provide this intensive face-to-face leadership training online.

The idea began as a seed and grew to become a full six-month online synchronous leadership development training. And while we achieved our goal of training another 25 employees, I have to say that the opportunity to refine and deliver the curriculum online for the first time was a surprising learning experience for me and extremely rewarding in the end for our participants. Do not allow the gravitational pull of getting to your destiny keep you from being antigravitational and enjoying the journey. Each challenge can become an opportunity for learning and growth, even the difficult challenges!

Fourth Practice Perspective: Leverage Serendipity

When I first began working as a case manager for a small nonprofit organization, I developed a close friendship with another case manager on the team. We would often attend meetings together and ultimately began socializing after work. During those times we would spend time talking about our work and our plans for the future. I remember being struck by the fact that he felt the agency was a dead-end place to work. He said, "There's not much going on here, with only four programs and just a few opportunities for promotion and professional development. I'm not sure how long I'm going to stick around." I recall being dumbfounded by his comments. "Really?" I replied, "I don't see it that way—in fact, I think there's a lot of potential here." He looked at me in the skeptical way people do when they feel they are a bit more in the know.

It was not long before he moved onto another case manager position with another nonprofit service organization, and just about the time he moved on, I was offered the opportunity to run my first program. I thought long and hard about the fact that we worked in the same place and shared similar skills and education, but I was the one who ended up with the opportunity to advance within the organization. Just dumb luck, right? Well, no, I don't think so. I think I *was* lucky but unlike my colleague I was also *ready* for the opportunity. The posture I took, that possibilities were quite present within the organization, laid the groundwork for me to jump on the chance to advance. I suspect that others too experienced my demeanor as one that would be receptive to the possibility of taking on a leadership role.

In 1854 Louis Pasteur was credited with saying that chance visits only the prepared mind. This astute comment, which was directed at the process of making observations within the realm of the natural sciences, aligns beautifully with an important perspective to hold within your leadership practice. By working to prepare yourself for possibilities you are ready to see the potential that exists and as a result seize a serendipitous moment. Good things happen when you prepare yourself for the possibilities. When we limit our view of the opportunity, we in turn shut ourselves off from the opportunity that appears.

Be sure to work at having a prepared mind!

Fifth Practice Perspective: Use a Compass, Not a Road Map

This fifth perspective comes to us with its share of simplexity. As you work to build your practice be sure that your strategies to develop yourself, your team, and your organization reflect an approach that is more directional in nature than it is hard and fast. Keeping your eye on the direction you hope to move in while avoiding the rigidity represented in a hard-and-fast, road map–based approach will become invaluable as you work to advance leadership practice. It is essential that you understand where you desire to be and what your vision is, yet be sure to remain flexible and adaptive as you encounter the many challenges and obstacles along the journey.

The trick here is to keep working toward the leadership vision that you have while building out just enough of the road map to remain flexible so that you can adapt to any twists and turns along the road. In many ways this is akin to the third practice perspective where you pay attention to the journey as well as the fourth practice perspective where *the way* you pay attention leaves you open to the possibilities that will present themselves.

In my work with developing leaders, I have seen times when they have become so committed to a particular path that their capacity to pivot has been hamstrung. It is fine to have a plan, but do not forget that the plan you develop is there to serve you. You should not feel that you must serve the plan. If the section of road that you have laid out is not working, then pay attention instead to the direction that you wish to pursue and feel free to change course. Remember, with a compass you will reach your destination, even if you get lost temporarily. Road maps, conversely, have limited utility, they become outdated, and there are plenty of opportunities to end up on a cul-de-sac.

Sixth Practice Perspective: Awareness

As a leader it is essential that you work to develop your own capacity for self-awareness. Awareness, however, can be a funny thing. Most people believe that they possess a high degree of self-awareness. Generally, the realization that one is lacking in awareness comes when someone points it out (and even then, we often resist taking this input) or in an instance when the individual is caught unaware. In a way awareness is like getting out on the ice in the winter. First you look to see if the ice seems thick enough and once you have determined it is "all good," then you venture out to the center of the pond. It is only when you start to hear the sound of cracking ice that you suddenly realize that you are in serious trouble and you've been caught unaware. You turn and run as quickly as possible, hoping and praying that you do not fall through.

Given the sometimes-allusive nature of awareness it is especially important to continually work to refine your own self-awareness as well as the awareness held by your team members. Meta-thinking is one way to help advance your own awareness. Meta-thinking is in effect thinking about thinking. Take time to consider what you are thinking and feeling and how your thoughts and feelings are connected to support or alternatively take away from the leadership practice you hope to develop.

Awareness can also be developed through effective feedback processes with colleagues, supervisors, and individuals whom you trust. Having the ability to seek and receive feedback provides a growing opportunity for you to expand your self-awareness. The best feedback is feedback that is solicited (you have asked for it), based on observation (about your work and/or performance), and nonjudgmental. It is also based on something that the receiver can do something about, it is checked for accuracy, and it is delivered in a way that is both timely and yet sensitive to the when and where. Giving feedback to someone in a large meeting about their performance is clearly less effective than providing the individual with the same information in a one-on-one meeting. Similarly, providing feedback in close proximity to the precipitating event or situation is more effective than putting it off.

Giving and receiving feedback can be challenging as it often requires that we work in an antigravitational way. Our culture often says "Forget about it" even though we know that feedback, when it is done well, will help the individual to develop their skills and capabilities. It is important to resist the temptation to put off providing feedback, or worse, to skip it because you have decided it is not worth the hassle. When you avoid feedback, you will soon see that things can go from bad to worse. Think for example of the splinter you have put off removing. It does not take long before you risk infection.

Seventh Practice Perspective: Address Inner Pressures

As you work to develop your self-awareness it is important to consider how your growing awareness connects to your inner self. From a psychoanalytic perspective we have thoughts and feelings as well as ideas about who we are in the world and how we should be, which all play a role in our leadership practice. If, for example, you believe that you must have things done right and done well 100 percent of the time, then your leadership will manifest itself in a manner that pursues perfection. Similarly, if you feel that you will never get it right, your capacity to develop a balanced sense of confidence will be hampered and your leadership practice will be adversely impacted.

Understanding your inner pressures and how to manage them successfully will help you to advance in your leadership ability. For example, my upbringing was within a White Anglo-Saxon Protestant family. Emotions were shared, but we largely adhered to the tradition in which one kept a "stiff upper lip." Angry and upset feelings were frowned upon. This seems innocuous enough, but let me tell you that as a leader I have had to learn how the internal pressure I experienced to avoid situations where people became emotional impacted my leadership practice. As my self-awareness grew, I began to realize that I would avoid confrontation or difficult situations simply because I found it intolerable to have people upset.

Ways to address your inner pressures start with first becoming aware that they exist. What types of inner pressure do you experience? Once you have taken stock and feel you know what they are, you can begin a process of addressing them. Sometimes this is as simple as being aware that you experience them and other times it may require that you develop a specific strategy to address the issue. In my case I had to practice managing the feelings that come with the expression of emotion by simply sitting rather than jumping into action to fix the situation. Trust me, as a strategy this was extremely hard, but in time I learned that holding fast rather than reacting would allow those involved to express themselves, they would feel heard, and the highly charged emotions would ultimately pass so that we might move the effort forward.

Another strategy that you can and should pursue is the use of supervision to help you work through the challenges that are presented vis-à-vis the inner pressures. Effective supervision can be critical in the development of any and all leadership strategies and is particularly helpful when you are working to address inner pressures. The key is to have a strong supervisor, something that is not always a readily apparent option. When this is not an option, I recommend finding a trusted individual to serve as a mentor for your leadership practice journey (see the section on finding a mentor later in this chapter).

Eighth Practice Perspective: Hero Leadership versus Leading Heroes

The eighth and final perspective that I recommend you take on is one more antigravitational effort that possesses enough in the way of dynamic layers to argue that it too meets the definition of simplexity. As you develop your leadership practice for yourself, your team, and your organization, be sure to take a stance that moves against the cultural grain of creating the lone hero leader. Instead, be sure to create heroes at all levels of the organization. Resist the urge to become a hero leader and ensure that each of your team members feels celebrated as a hero for their contribution to the organization's mission and vision.

If you allow yourself to become the hero leader, then, by definition, you will exclude others from having the ability to share in leadership practice. When a team member feels that there is no room for them to play an important role there is a natural tendency for them to stand down rather than take on leadership behavior and engage in action that helps to buoy the work of the organization. Celebrate all the team member contributions and work to give credit away to those who are working on the team. By taking this stance you support the very fabric of your team's commitment and engagement. Grabbing the glory for oneself feels wonderful in the moment, but sadly squanders the value that can come from team members feeling that their contribution has made a difference. It is essential that each team member feels that they, too, can be a leader and have a role to play in helping to advance the organization.

By creating heroes across the organization, you also build your team's capacity to be engaged and responsive to the needs of the organization. Nonprofit organizations that enhance successful leadership practice across and within the organization are agencies that become resilient and find that they are well equipped to be successful in the face of any challenges that occur.

Each of the eight practice perspectives can help you to develop your own efficacy as a leader. In the Appendix of this book, you will find a tool for conducting a self-assessment of your abilities in each of the practice perspectives. The tool, in addition to helping you conduct a self-assessment, also makes it possible for you to thoughtfully develop strategies to advance your scoring and ultimately your capabilities in each of the areas. Once you have gone through and scored yourself, take some time to identify specific steps that you will take to heighten your skills within each practice perspective. I recommend using your assessment as a working document and revisiting it from time to time to see how your practice perspectives are developing.

Another option for the use of this tool is to work with your team to have each team member complete an assessment. Once everyone has completed their assessment, take time to share as a group where each individual scores. What strengths do they have and where are the areas for growth? What are some of the strategies that everyone has come up with to move their practice perspectives forward? Often working together as a team on practice perspectives can help leverage your group's ability to exercise collective leadership skills. As a group you will develop a greater understanding of everyone's strengths, how they contribute effectively to the team, and where the areas for growth lie. Most teams quickly realize that they can complement each other and help to support their colleagues as they work to advance their leadership practice.

Strategies for Developing Leadership Practice

Now that we have looked at the eight leadership practice perspectives, our attention turns to some specific strategies for developing leadership practice. The strategies explored in this section of Chapter 2 are not intended to be exhaustive, but rather representative of tried-and-true ways to help develop your leadership practice. As with the earlier discourse you should consider each of these strategies as dynamic and as such consider that they apply to your personal leadership practice as well as your team's and your organization's leadership capacity.

Opportunity and Engagement

My own research in leadership development discussed in depth in Chapter 5 shows that leadership skills and abilities will grow when opportunities are present to take on leadership responsibilities. Actively pursuing opportunities for developing your leadership practice aligns closely with your engagement with the organization and taken together they can be a powerful source for leadership development. Given this, use your practice perspectives to be on the hunt for opportunities to advance your leadership skills. On any given day, if you avail yourself, you will find there are multiple instances that can serve as an opportunity to develop your leadership skills. This can be something as simple as volunteering to serve on a committee, being willing to take on a specific responsibility for the team such as organizing an event, agreeing to take minutes, offering to pursue a fundraiser, or any number of activities, including representing the organization with external stakeholders.

If you are willing to step up and take it on, then you will quickly see that your fellow team members—including your supervisors—no matter the level, will begin to gravitate toward you and think of you as a go-to person for activities that can lend themselves to additional leadership responsibility and, more important, your capacity to develop as a leader. Actively pursuing opportunities to develop your leadership skills will provide you with invaluable experience so that you can practice and refine your leadership skills.

For example, I can think of a newly minted entry-level leader within a nonprofit multiservice agency who was seen volunteering for any number of activities. First, he offered to keep track of his program's monthly vehicle safety checklist. From there his director asked him if he wanted to serve as the safety coordinator, representing his program for the agency's corporate safety committee. Soon the committee discovered that he had graphic design skills and he began churning out a wonderful safety committee newsletter—while along the way being promoted to assistant director. It was clear that he not only possessed leadership skills but was actively refining them while building his reputation as a go-to person. He is on a journey, and it will be interesting to see where the journey takes him.

Pursuing opportunity and working to be fully engaged not only benefits the individual, but also the entire team. In my formal leadership role, I know that creating multiple opportunities for employees to be engaged and to develop their own leadership capabilities not only helps them learn and grow but also benefits the organization. An organization that has multiple opportunities for employees to develop and express leadership is an organization that is vibrant and dynamic.

Nonprofit agencies, when organized well, can help to ensure that there are multiple opportunities for employees to become engaged in developing their leadership capabilities. Clearly there are the traditional notions of leadership training programs which in and of themselves have a positive impact, and then there are a multitude of other strategies that can help to build your organization's culture of leadership development. As mentioned, committees are an easy way to help people develop their leadership capacity. In particular, ad hoc committees that are working to address a particular project can be useful as a strategy to connect employees to a level of leadership practice. There are other structural strategies as well. For example, how the organization pursues its continuous quality improvement (CQI) practices can help or hinder the development of leadership practice. Is the effort pursued by a single department or employee or is there cross-organization participation for employees at various levels within the agency? Providing opportunities for various parts of the organization to work together on functions beyond the individual's day-to-day responsibilities makes it possible for individuals to step up and take responsibility that not only benefits the organization but also helps the employee build their own leadership practice.

For example, rather than simply relying on a quality improvement director, you might develop a peer-review process that engages interdisciplinary team members from across the organization to share in continuous quality improvement visits, CQI goals, and objectives as well as practices. In this way there are multiple opportunities for employee engagement and leadership development that are built into the organization's practices.

Strategies of this type can be pursued across the organization, covering various agency functions. From continuous quality improvement practices to employee training and development to information technology to events planning, the use of systems that provide the framework for employees of the organization to pursue opportunities to develop their leadership capacity are many. As an individual, watch for these opportunities; as a leader within an organization, strive to optimize the number that are available, knowing that done well these opportunities will build leadership practice across the organization.

Become an Advocate for Leadership Development Practice

As you strive to pursue as well as enhance your organization's leadership and engagement opportunities, I want to be sure that you prepare yourself to become a wholly committed advocate. An advocate not only for your own leadership practice but also at an organizational level as well. Building leadership practice for yourself and for the team is something that must be intentional and the desire to develop yourself and the team around you must be articulated. Advocates give voice to a cause that without their public support might not become a reality. Similarly, you must give voice to the desire to develop your leadership skills. This is true as well for those who hope to grow leadership capacity within the organization.

I recall early on in my career having the flawed belief that if I worked hard and developed myself that someone would notice, and I would be provided with greater leadership responsibility. It did not take long before I realized that no one truly noticed. They did appreciate all that I would do, but simply thought I was content with the status quo and had no idea that I had a vision of where my leadership journey might go. Once I started to say affirmatively that I desired to grow as a leader and have greater responsibility, then people began to intentionally consider how I could contribute to new efforts that would represent a greater and more in-depth leadership role.

It is also critical to advocate for leadership practice across the entire organization. If you do not articulate the importance of everyone developing their capacity to share in leadership practice, then you will have a hard time establishing an agencywide leadership development perspective. Other norms or patterns of behavior can take hold that could ultimately hurt the agency's capacity to be a place that is vibrant and, as Raelin (2011) would say, *Leaderful*.

Within organizational life there are multiple places where your advocacy can pay off. Annual evaluations become a time when future goals and professional development can be clearly articulated. If you desire future leadership responsibility and growth this is a perfect place to articulate how you hope to grow. Regular meetings with your supervisor become a natural place to talk about future goals as well as professional growth and development. Consider training opportunities that are geared toward your leadership development, as well.

As you pursue each of these strategies, recall the practice perspectives we explored earlier in this chapter. Be sure to have the long view in mind, do not forget to enjoy the journey, remember to use your compass to stay focused on your True North, and be sure to leverage serendipity. For example, you might say if you write about your desire to have more leadership responsibility in your annual evaluation that your current supervisor will see this as a threat. First, my condolences for having a supervisor with this view, but beyond that recognize that this individual is a point in time in your journey and there are other strategies to pursue in your development. While you will encounter obstacles in your leadership journey, your practice perspectives make it possible to pivot around just such a barrier. We know because we have taken the long view that our tenacious nature will help to overcome each challenge that is encountered.

Find a Mentor

Early on in my career I quickly realized that there was much to learn from more senior leaders within my nonprofit organization. Some of this learning came naturally by observing their approach and style to any number of situations. I learned from their example both what to do and, at times, what not to do. Often my direct supervisor served as a source of leadership development, particularly when I had a supervisor who had leadership strengths. This was ideal because meetings were regularly scheduled and included discussions about various situations that had arisen between meeting times. There were times, though, when my direct supervisor was not someone I felt I could learn from. In these instances, I felt their skills as a leader were lacking. These were the instances where I would typically learn what *not* to do. A reverse role model, if you will.

When I found myself in this predicament, I realized that I would have to seek support for my developmental leadership journey from someone other than my direct supervisor. It was not too difficult to look around the organization or even outside of the agency to find someone with the skills and expertise in leadership that I could respect. The key was to be intentional about this effort to pursue a mentor who could support my development. There is always a risk that you could become complacent by resigning yourself to the fact that you have a difficult situation with a supervisor, and rather than pursue an external mentor and coach, settle into feeling stuck. Better to be intentional and avoid the cul-de-sac of complacency as you work to develop your leadership capability.

I have heard and experienced the idea as well that mentees choose their mentor. If you are to have a mentor, and you should, set about intentionally developing a professional relationship with a colleague or associate whom you respect. In time this respect can form the foundation for building a relationship of trust, support, and learning that in the best of worlds will become reciprocal over time.

The positive impact associated with a true mentor relationship is well documented. Ayoobzadeh and Boies (2020), for example, researched the impact of mentors and found that successful mentor relationships helped to increase positive outcomes for the participants. Now notice that the key term here is *successful mentor relationship*. It is not enough to simply participate in a structured mentor program within your organization and assume that the mentor/mentee relationship will be defined as successful. There are many variables that come into play when we pursue a successful mentor relationship—not the least of which revolves around the way in which the organization's culture supports the development of mentorships (Johnson & Smith, 2019).

Considerations include whether there is mutually shared respect between the mentor and the mentee. The mentor must be perceived by the mentee as having the skills necessary to play the role in a positive way and even beyond that it is critical that the mentor have the skill set necessary to fulfill the role of mentor. And even if these pieces are in place it's essential that the mentor and the mentee have a willingness to develop and sustain a supportive relationship All these variables and more are at play in the development of a successful mentor relationship.

It might be that your pursuit of a mentor will move you beyond the single mentor/mentee relationship to consider having multiple mentor relationships, where you can draw support and guidance from several individuals in your network of relationships. No matter the form, be sure to develop a mentor/mentee relationship. Be intentional in this area as the rewards for your leadership development will be significant.

Sharpen Your Saw

There is an old proverb about a man who was working furiously to saw down a tree. A farmer passing by could not help but notice the man, who was covered head to toe in sweat and nearing collapse. The farmer asked the man how long he had been at the task of sawing down the tree. The man replied that he had been on the job for hours and thought that the tree must be the hardest of wood. As the farmer leaned in, he saw that the teeth on the saw were dull and nearly undetectable. "Maybe you should sharpen your saw," the farmer commented. The man looked dumbfounded as he had only considered how remarkably hard the wood was on this tree, not the state of his saw.

Leadership tools, like any tool, require sharpening. You may have developed a complete toolbox for your leadership practice, but have you taken the time to ensure that your tools are well maintained? If not, you will find yourself like the gentleman in the proverb, working all day to no avail.

Sharpening your saw from a leadership perspective can involve a wide array of activities. Attending trainings is one way to fine-tune your capacity to use your leadership practice tools. Reading and exposing yourself to emergent ideas as well as tried-and-true notions of effective leadership practice can also serve as an important source for sharpening your proverbial saw. Find a community to talk about leadership and take time to read about leadership practice. There are any number of leadership groups and forums that exist on multiple platforms—LinkedIn, for example—as well as various leadership associations, such as ILA, the International Leadership Association. Be active and pursue membership in these forums so that you ensure that your leadership development is something that is ongoing.

You can also pursue more informal ways to develop your leadership practice. For example, I have a group of colleagues who meet monthly to share ideas about leadership and management practice. This group has become invaluable and serves a function that is helpful well beyond our monthly meetings by making it possible to reach out and connect about specific challenges between meetings.

Another way to sharpen your saw is to develop your ability to be mindful and fully present in your leadership practice. Mindfulness practice has become an important habit for many successful leaders. We are busy within our culture, constantly going somewhere and always doing something. Taking time to slow down, stop, and be in the moment helps you to build your capacity to be reflective. If you can calm the noise in your head that is created by our frenetic pace, then you will be better able to exercise leadership practice that supports your efforts. In the Appendix of this book, you will find five mindfulness practices that are both easy and simple to practice.

My go-to mindfulness practice from this list is mindful breathing. It is an activity that I can do in just a few minutes, sitting at my desk or just before I enter a meeting, that helps to enhance my mindfulness and ultimately my effectiveness.

You might feel that you do not have time to pursue a mindfulness practice or that you do not see why this would be important. It is important to understand that research has shown the efficacy of mindfulness. Chin et al. (2019), for example, underscore how mindfulness is associated with stress reduction. Similarly, Bell's (2015) research shows that people who are more mindful have better physical and mental health, including less anxiety and lower blood pressure. Each of the findings here underscore how mindfulness can help you build your leadership capability. The importance of mindfulness in leadership is also underscored by the work of Tohme and Joseph (2020), whose research identified a positive correlation between authenticity, mindfulness, and emotional intelligence.

Taken together these activities can help to ensure that you continually refine your ability to make wise use of your leadership toolbox. Do not be caught working yourself to death with dull tools. Work intentionally to enhance your leadership practice at every turn. I am confident that you will find the various activities associated with sharpening your leadership practice to be enjoyable as well as rewarding. Remember this journey is one that should be ongoing. We can and should work every day to advance our leadership skills.

3

Choosing a Leadership Style

As we work through our plan to advance your efficacy as a leader and a manager, it is important to dedicate some of the discourse to consider the question of leaders versus managers. Throughout this book the term *leader* is used interchangeably with the term *manager*. The reason for this is born of my view about the role of leaders and the role of managers. If you take time to explore the literature surrounding both terms, you will quickly see that most authors take a position that is best illustrated by the old saying, "Managers do things right while leaders do the right thing." Many authors argue that leadership and management are two distinct practices and as a result they should be explored separately.

My view is contrary to this, believing instead that management and leadership exist together. Each should be viewed as being couched with the other. For reasons that you will see in Chapter 4, as we explore the role of culture in leadership practice it is not enough to focus solely on leadership while forgoing any consideration of your managerial capabilities. Being an effective leader requires that you develop as an effective manager, and being effective as a manager requires that you develop leadership capability. Leadership capability and managerial capability are hand in glove and together they constitute effective leadership practice. Given this lens, it's important as we begin to explore your leadership style that we keep an eye on the role that managerial skills play in your leadership approach.

In the next few pages we will take a 1,000-foot view of leadership approaches that are widely written about and explored within the field of leadership. Some will readily appeal to you while others may spark less interest. It is important, however, to have some understanding of what leadership approaches or styles are present and how they either connect or not to your own tendency as a leader. As a leader you will want to settle on one strategy over another with the understanding that it's perfectly appropriate to draw from a number of leadership approaches.

After a brief exploration of leadership approaches, we then settle in for a more in-depth review of servant leadership as developed by Robert Greenleaf (1977). The reason for taking a more in-depth view of servant leadership is because of its alignment with nonprofit leadership practice and the important service-centered values that typically form the core of nonprofit organizations. In addition, there is a widely held view that servant leadership can help you build connections with your employees and fellow team members (see, for example, Blanchard & Brodwell, 2018).

Transactional Leadership

Transactional leadership is likely one of the older forms of leadership practice. The focus within this form of leadership lies in its name, in particular the fact that behavior within the leader/follower relationship is driven by a system of rewards and consequences. Within this form of leadership practice motivation is driven by a leadership that rewards performance and in turn can punish poor performance by withholding rewards or pursuing consequences. Consider, for example, a common practice in law firms that rewards attorneys financially for achieving a certain number of billable hours during the course of the business year. Car dealerships also utilize a more transactional leadership approach by rewarding salespeople for achieving sales quotas. In both instances employees can lose their positions if they do not meet targeted performance criteria. In the purest sense, the transactional leader is unconcerned with how you are doing— whether you are invested, engaged, and growing as an employee— and is focused instead on motivating you to pursue rewards and avoid consequences.

Nonprofit organizations typically look askance at transactional leadership practice, yet it's important to consider how, despite this view, there are always elements of transactional leadership practice present. For example, consider the billable hour standards that typically come with per diem case management roles or many outpatient clinicians. In these instances, employees are expected to meet these requirements to avoid some form of consequence and remain in the good graces of their employer. Similarly, unless you are a volunteer in a nonprofit organization, you receive a paycheck for your efforts; in a very basic way this is a transaction centered on "If you do this, we'll do that"—a sort of quid pro quo. The point is that even if you choose not to utilize a transactional leadership approach there are circumstances where transactional elements are present.

Transformational Leadership

Transformational leaders in contrast to transactional leaders are extremely concerned with their employees' growth and development. They hope to have each employee become better able to pursue their role and responsibilities and they hope for their team members' development. This is typically a primary concern for the transformational leader, and they achieve this by sharing their passion for the work at hand. Transformational leaders are inspirational, and they spend time sharing the vision they hold for the organization as well as the employee.

Transformational leaders take time to ensure that their employees have the opportunity to take on more, learn more, and grow within their work and responsibilities. A transformational leader will celebrate the promotion of an employee even when it means that they move on to another part of the organization or leave the organization altogether. Their overriding concern, as you would expect, is transformation, moving from one level to a higher, more developed state.

Charismatic Leadership

Charismatic leaders are leaders who have personality and charm; they possess a huge presence and because of this people are drawn to them. Because of their dynamic presence they can engage employees and develop a following. Often people are eager to work for a charismatic leader and they appreciate how being in their inner circle can benefit them. In addition, the charismatic leader often becomes central to the organization's image.

Many would argue that this type of leadership is one where you either have it or you do not. Big personalities with a high degree of charm and the presence that can draw people to follow them typically have traits that help support them in this way. It can be difficult to learn how to develop a personality that helps people to be drawn to you. Despite this, however, there are things that one can learn if you would like to be more charismatic in your approach. Charm and public speaking skills are both examples of charismatic leader attributes that can be refined.

As you've no doubt noted there are overlaps between the various leadership styles. For example, you can think about transformational leaders you have worked with and I am sure you will agree that they were quite charismatic in many ways; the difference, though, is in how they focus their leadership practice. Transformational leaders want you to develop and grow. Charismatic leaders, however, are more concerned with using their charm and the huge presence that is their personality to lead employees and the larger organization.

Quiet Leadership

The quiet leadership practice is juxtaposed to the charismatic leadership style. Quiet leaders work without any sign of a big ego. They work from the background to help advance the mission of the organization.

They are seen to consistently push for the team's recognition while readily taking responsibility for any shortcomings that are encountered.

True quiet leaders are quite rare in Western culture. Our obsession with the single hero leader within organizational life often results in a negative assessment of a quiet leader. One might ask "Why doesn't he take a stand?" when in fact quiet leaders are not abdicating their responsibilities, they are just working quietly to ensure there is a successful outcome for the organization and the team.

I have known several quiet leaders during my work with nonprofit organizations. I am always struck by how the esteem in which I hold them grows over time. A true quiet leader is so quiet that you find yourself wondering whether they are truly leading at all. In time you come to realize that they are very active, but in a way that doesn't draw attention to themselves, instead preferring to help build and resource the team as well as the organization to ensure success.

Even if you were to decide that your propensity for leadership practice is not aligned with a quiet leadership style, there are elements of this type of leadership that are particularly powerful. Supporting and celebrating the team above your own interests, for example, is an important strategy that helps to support the idea that we need to build heroes on our team rather than become the team's hero. The idea that developing resources so that your team can excel is also an important notion. Many teams fall short not because they are incapable, but rather because they have been underresourced for the task at hand.

Situational Leadership

I hear from many of my students and from my leadership trainees that they like the idea of situational leadership. A situational leader is a leader who regularly scans the environment in order to fully understand the current context and then devise a plan of action. They have the ability to adjust their leadership style based on what is happening in the operating environment and adapt quickly in order to ensure success.

To be effective as a situational leader, you must fully know your team's capability. You have to have the ability to organize a plan for action and know when to push, pull, or stand by. Timing and a full understanding of a given situation is of essence. For example, I have watched strong situational leaders do extremely well during the current pandemic. They are able to mobilize their team, develop practices and policies that can effectively respond to the changing environment brought about by COVID-19, and then pivot as needed.

Situational leaders have the ability to move between the traditional leadership styles of autocratic, democratic, and laissez-faire leadership. A situational leader knows when to tell you what to do, just as they understand when it is time to join you in getting it done. It is an effective leadership style, though it does require that the given leader have a strong awareness of the current context as well as the skills to pivot between various approaches.

Servant Leadership

As noted earlier in this chapter I believe that servant leadership is well aligned with the work we pursue within nonprofit organizations. A servant leader believes that the primary purpose behind their leadership practice is to be in service to the organization, to others on the team, and to the larger society. Servant leaders work to improve the good of all and they feel that their job is to transform others as well, helping them to be in service to the organization and the wider good. This approach as described by Robert Greenleaf (1977) has 10 core characteristics, each of which come together to form the basis for effective servant leadership practice. I explore the 10 characteristics associated with servant leadership next; there is an assessment tool within the Appendix so that you can score your own capabilities in each of the categories.

Listening

Listening is the first of the 10 characteristics that form the basis for effective servant leadership. It makes sense that listening is the first skill to focus on, particularly since we know how important it is for employees and team members to feel truly heard. An effective leader is a leader who pursues deep listening with their employees. Having the ability to stop and provide your full attention to truly hear what is being said is extremely important.

We live in a time of hustle and bustle; we are always going somewhere and doing something. Technology too has caused multiple distractions in our lives. Just try having a conversation with someone who has an iPhone or smartphone open in their hand. To listen we must expand our capacity to quiet ourselves and fully focus our attention on the individual or individuals and what they are trying to say to us.

Included in this is the ability to listen to what is being said and what is *not* being said. Often what is not being said is at the heart of the interaction. Servant leaders develop a capacity to hear the unspoken and to carefully shed light on what is not being said. I can recall a time when a teammate continually reached out to me. Each time the discourse seemed to be about something quite trivial. It was the type of conversation that makes you wonder what it was really about as each time the questions seemed trivial, the kind that one can quickly answer for oneself. As I thought about the interactions, I realized that something else must have been going on. Once I had this revelation, I called to say that I had been thinking about our last two conversations and wondered now if there was something else that I could help with. It was as if a dam had opened as the team member shared their concerns with a fellow employee. Listening to what is being said as well as what is not being said is extremely important.

Empathy

Empathy is closely related to deep listening, as it is critical to truly understanding what is going on with your team member. Empathy is the capacity to fully understand the other person's experience. Of course, this is distinct from feeling sympathy for someone, as sympathy suggests a position of privilege over someone as you feel bad for them. To have empathy is to suspend your own experience and instead immerse yourself in an effort to understand what the individual is experiencing. Suspending your own experience can be a challenge particularly as we begin to listen to what the other individual is saying. It is simply human nature to want to relate your experience with what you are hearing, but to do that is to block your ability to fully know what your team member is experiencing.

Empathy within servant leadership goes beyond simply understanding a situation or circumstance that is being shared with you. Empathy in this context is having the ability to understand the individual as a whole person: to be able to know their experience and appreciate it from their perspective. For example, your team member might be a supervisee or colleague and they are also someone who has their own personal challenges, hopes, and dreams. Seeing each person as a whole person and understanding their lived experience helps leverage your capacity to be effective as a servant leader. Having the ability to truly exercise empathy helps to buoy your capacity with regard to the other characteristics that are part and parcel of this leadership style.

Healing

Servant leaders work hard to support team members in working through challenges they encounter and to help resolve problems and conflicts that naturally arise within organizational life. They recognize the importance of working through issues that people have within the team and know that interpersonal struggles, left unattended, will result in greater strife and division. A central element of this desire to resolve conflict and address problems that employees experience rests in the idea that the best organizational culture is a culture that is free from fear. Fear can be a driving force in organizational discord. Conflicts in fear-based organizational or team cultures are driven underground, and people withdraw from engagement. In contrast a culture that is free of fear is a culture that allows participants to be more open and willing to have issues and challenges come to the surface so that they can be worked through.

Servant leaders pay attention to strategies to lower what I call the fear factor. They do this by modeling a willingness to refrain from judgment, to encourage open and honest communication, and to set a tone that supports learning and growth. As a part of this they create space for employees to make mistakes and reinforce those who come forward to share the mistakes they have made and what they have learned from the given misstep. In a very real way servant leaders provide room for forgiveness, which in turn helps to encourage thoughtful risk taking on the part of the employee or team member.

Each of these characteristics naturally builds upon the other and is interdependent. Deep listening combined with true empathy helps employees to feel heard and understood, which in turn sets the stage for a team or organizational culture that is ready to solve problems and work through conflict. As a team becomes able to work through conflicts they heal, and as they heal, they build their capacity to work through future challenges. Like a broken bone that has been properly set, the spot where the break occurred is stronger. Effectively working through conflict is a way to create a stronger team.

Awareness

Just as we noted in the practice perspectives for leadership development servant leadership also believes that awareness is an important characteristic. Servant leadership builds on the important notion of self-awareness to include the importance of awareness that is integrated and holistic. While it's critically important to be self-aware, it is also essential that your awareness goes beyond the self to include awareness of the dynamics that are present around you. This level of awareness includes dynamics present within other individuals on your team, the team as a whole, the organization, and the external operating environment. Developing awareness at this level is multilayered and dynamic and like the other characteristics is one that you will want to continually develop. Each of the many layers is ever-changing, as we as individuals continue our developmental path, our team members change, and the operating environment is ever shifting. Given this, it is important to work hard at maintaining and developing your capacity for awareness. Keep sharpening your saw by exposing yourself to new opportunities, practice mindfulness, and stay connected within and throughout your organization and the surrounding community. The more aware you are at these varying levels, the better able you will be to leverage effective leadership.

As an extension of this I would suggest that you also develop the capacity within your practice to leverage your employees' awareness. Team members who have developed heightened awareness of self, their team, the organization, and the surrounding community are team members who are prepared to join you in pursing effective leadership practice. This is true as well for all the servant leadership characteristics. As we know, a rising tide lifts all boats, and a team that shares a holistic and integrated level of awareness is a team that is better equipped to support the organization's mission and vision going forward.

Persuasion

Sometimes people confuse persuasion with coercion. Other times persuasion gets confused with a sales strategy and hence is seen as distasteful by some. In the context of servant leadership, the capacity to utilize persuasion is seen more appropriately as an expression of the leader's commitment to the mission, vision, values, and beliefs of the organization. In this context there is nothing "used-car salesmen"-like about their efforts. Persuasion is not an attempt to trick or convince someone to buy into something that is a sleight of hand. Quite to the contrary, the servant leader is working to be sure you understand the importance of what they believe. They want you to share fervently in what they believe is at the heart of the organization's work.

A servant leader believes to their core in the importance of the work that is being done and because of this they want internal as well as external stakeholders to share their view. This is where the importance of persuasion lies. In fact, servant leaders feel so strongly about the importance of the work that the organization is engaged in that they are willing to actively engage with internal as well as external stakeholders to help them fully understand the importance of the organization's work.

Those around the servant leader find that they know exactly where the leader stands on important aspects of the organization such as the agency's mission, the vision for the future, and the values that the organization holds near and dear to their everyday work. There is a genuineness and authenticity that emanates from the servant leader that is bound to their commitment to engage in persuasion.

Conceptualization

Servant leaders have the capacity to see beyond the day-to-day work of the organization. They have the ability to step back and see the larger picture. They successfully resist the distractions that might cause a loss of focus and they are able to keep a healthy vision for the organization in play. Their capacity for ensuring a strong vision extends beyond the organization and includes a vision for themselves from a professional and personal standpoint. Servant leaders strive to be grounded in their professional sense of self, where they desire to be and how they hope to be from a personal standpoint.

The gravitational pull of the day-to-day pressures that confront leaders is strong and so it is important to leverage the practice perspectives we have explored to help you stay on track with this leadership characteristic. For example, striving to be antigravitational, leveraging awareness, addressing inner pressures, and holding onto the long view are all strategies that will help you continue to build and enhance your capacity to engage in conceptualization as well as any number of the characteristics central to servant leadership.

Foresight

One might say that foresight is a close cousin of conceptualization. The nuance here is that your leadership skills include the capacity to understand the consequences and outcomes associated with a plan of action. Thinking critically about the road forward for you, your team, or the larger organization is extremely important. Foresight, for example, includes the ability to consider any number of possibilities that lay before you.

Foresight is developed through your own personal and professional development as you integrate your experiences within the nonprofit field. Learning from each experience is critically important to developing your capacity to conceptualize the potential that exists in the road ahead. Awareness also works hand in glove with the learning process. Integrating the lessons while engaging in meta-thinking makes it possible to heighten your capacity for foresight.

Stewardship

As stewards, servant leaders know that they work to help enhance the team and the organization's ability to pursue the agency's mission. A true steward takes the view that they are entrusted with protecting the organization, to help in any way possible to advance the work of the agency. They also know that they do not own the operation but rather take the position that their job is to promote, protect, and preserve the resources that are bound together to form the entity.

Stewardship is reflected in the way in which servant leaders pursue their responsibilities and in the way in which they present themselves to the team, the larger organization, and to outside stakeholders. They do not aggrandize themselves; they are careful to use the organization's resources prudently and they fully understand that their job is to someday pass the organization on to the next leader as the agency pursues its critical mission.

Commitment to Growth

Like a transformational leader, servant leaders are committed to the ongoing growth and development of their team members. They believe firmly that everyone has the potential to develop further, to become more skilled to learn and to grow. This commitment to growth is manifest in the way that they talk, engage with their team members, and in the practices and policies they support and help develop.

Their commitment to growth extends beyond the immediate team or supervisees to the entire organization. In addition, they exemplify a commitment to growth in the way that they also personally pursue their own development. They set an example for all team members about the importance of developing one's skills and abilities, and through this they give permission for all team members to continue to learn. It is important not to underestimate the importance of this characteristic and the role that it plays in helping to build a learning organization in which the entire culture emphasizes the importance of personal and professional growth.

As you work to develop your own leadership practice, it is important to consider how you manifest your commitment to growth. Are you, for example, open to continually refining and developing your professional skills? Does this interest extend beyond your own personal and professional growth to include the growth of others around you? These are important questions that translate into action, which in turn helps to grow your capacity in this important area.

Commitment to Building Strong Community

Each of the servant leadership characteristics helps to provide the foundation for realizing this important characteristic: the presence of a true commitment to building a strong community. A commitment to building a strong community goes beyond the immediate team and the organization to include the larger community. It is widely understood that strong communities serve as a source of resilience for individual members. The more resilient one is, the better able the individual, team, or organization will be at bouncing back from difficult challenges.

The work that we do in the nonprofit sector is extremely challenging and the importance of having a strong community to support the ongoing efforts of the organization cannot be stressed enough. I recall for example the impact that my team members felt when a young woman that we were working with tried to kill herself. The team member who found her with her wrists cut was able to rise to the occasion and get her to emergency services, but the aftermath, the impact upon the individual staff members, could have been devastating had it not been for the fact that we had such a strong community and support was readily available. The development of a strong community provides an incredible return to the organization and is integral to servant leadership practice.

Taken together the 10 characteristics of servant leadership provide an important way of thinking about your leadership practice. Each of the characteristics align nicely with the work we pursue within our respective nonprofit organizations. And while each characteristic has its own merit in pursuit of effective leadership, they also work in a complementary way to help you advance your impact as a nonprofit manager and leader. For example, having the capacity to listen, truly listen in a deep and meaningful way, when combined with the ability to truly empathize with another helps to open the door toward effective conflict resolution. Healing within the team is more readily available when team members feel heard and fully understood.

In a like manner your ability to develop conceptualization and foresight is directly connected to your capacity to be aware. As we have discussed, becoming aware at multiple levels, personally, professionally, at an individual and interpersonal level, supports your ability to see the big picture and to anticipate how circumstances may unfold. In each case we see that the characteristics which form the basis for servant leadership have their own merit and are complementary and interconnected.

I have included a tool in the Appendix that you can use as a self-assessment for your capability in each of the 10 characteristics. If you are interested in developing your skills in this leadership style, I recommend that you take a few minutes to complete the assessment. Once you have considered your score for the individual characteristics, consider what strategies you would use to pursue moving the score a bit higher. The strategies to advance your score do not have to be too complex. Oftentimes it is enough to say that you want to work on a particular characteristic in order to move the needle forward and raise your score. For example, I know that I should work on my ability to listen carefully. Sometimes I am too caught up in what I'm planning to accomplish or what I'm in the midst of doing. By recognizing that I need to raise my score in the characteristic of listening, I find that this new awareness makes it possible for me to be more mindful, to stop what I am doing and truly listen.

Other strategies that you can develop might require some more specific action steps. For example, if you want to advance the characteristic of healing, which involves problem solving and conflict resolution, I recommend that you take some time and read some of the literature about the power of forgiveness in organizational life, or perhaps read some articles on conflict management. Other options might include attending a training to advance your ability.

Now you may have read this section and decided that you would prefer to pursue one of the other leadership styles identified. This is perfectly appropriate. The important point here is that you begin to consider how you would like your leadership practice to manifest itself. What kind of leadership style connects most closely to how you think of yourself and your individual skills? As I have noted, servant leadership aligns nicely with nonprofit leadership and management, but this is not the only type of leadership that aligns nicely with nonprofit work. Transformational leadership, situational leadership, and quiet leadership also align nicely with the work of nonprofit managers and leaders. The key is to decide on a leadership approach that most appeals to you and then apply yourself to developing the tools necessary to advance your leadership practice. Remember, this is a journey and your leadership development should be viewed in this light as opposed to a final destination.

Emergent Thought in Leadership Practice

To this point I have written largely about leadership models that are focused on the actions of the individual leader. The history of leadership practice and leadership development efforts as well have largely focused on strategies to enhance the individual's ability to lead. Given this, leadership models have concerned themselves with identifying the skills required for the individual to become successful as a leader. Naturally, there is value in considering how you can develop your ability to lead an organization, but to stay singularly focused on the individual actor is to ignore the dynamic nature of leadership practice within nonprofit organizations.

There is a growing number of theorists as well as practitioners who have taken a step back from the single-actor model of leadership to instead consider the importance of leadership activity that occurs across and within the entire organization. Leadership done well is done in collaboration, in which every individual within the organization can and should fulfill a leadership role at various times for various purposes. Within this context we recognize the importance of helping to foster leadership behavior and practice across the organization. A nonprofit organization that has a team that is highly committed to the mission, vision, and values of the agency, that is willing to step into leadership activity, is an incredibly dynamic and powerful organization. In contrast, an organization that waits for the positional leader to tell people what to do is an organization that will struggle in today's complex operating environment.

There are a variety of theorists who write about these emergent leadership ideas. Joe Raelin (2003), for example, is recognized for his leaderful practice model. Raelin believes that the most effective organizations are the ones that can develop leaderful practice throughout the agency. From his perspective, leaderfulness is manifest through the presence of four primary tenets. To be leaderful, leadership needs to be concurrent, collective, collaborative, and compassionate. This is in contrast to traditional leadership, which is seen to be more serial, individual, controlling, and dispassionate in nature.

Other theorists who concern themselves with the dynamic and interrelated nature of leadership include the Pierce and Conger (2003) model of shared leadership, which describes how leadership, as a social phenomenon, exists throughout the strata of the organization. In their shared leadership model the focus is on continual learning for success. Distributed leadership as developed by Spillane (2006) connects with both leaderful practice and shared leadership in recognizing that leadership involves the interaction between a network of individuals who can draw on expertise that is available and as needed without being concerned about boundaries and silos created by department and traditional organizational structure.

As Chapter 5 shows, I have come to see the importance of building leadership practice outside the metes and bounds of the single actor. The conceptual frame that I have developed, called *generative leadership*, shares the importance of understanding that leadership is a process, one that is closely connected to the engagement of the entire team and the larger organization. Truly effective leadership is leadership that exists beyond the individual and instead takes into consideration the capacity for the development of leadership practice at all levels within the organization's structure.

It is true that we need to develop our individual leadership skills and abilities and it is equally as important that we pursue strategies to enhance the leadership capacity across and at all levels within the organization itself. This in many ways is the secret sauce that will help determine your success as a leader, as well as the ongoing success of the entire enterprise. In summary, I encourage you to consider applying the strategies explored to extend beyond your own development to include your team and the entire organization.

A Classic Frame

As we consider the nature of your leadership style, I would be remiss if I didn't share a model for decision making that I have found particularly helpful. It is a classic approach developed by Tannenbaum and Schmidt (1973) that is extremely helpful when it comes to making decisions within the context of a team and the larger organization.

In their work they identify strategies for choosing a leadership style based on a number of key variables present within the team, the operating environment, the organization's culture, and the larger culture. The leadership styles are seen as operating on a continuum between an autocratic approach and democratic approach to leadership style. In between these ends of the continuum are gradations of each.

Over time I have simplified their approach to include four basic strategies for managers when choosing a leadership approach.

Consistent with Tannenbaum and Schmidt's approach, the appropriateness of each strategy is grounded in variables that are drawn from the existing context. For example, some strategies take more time and so the use of a more time-intensive strategy would be inappropriate if you did not have the time necessary to make the decision. Another variable has to do with the skills and abilities that are present within the team. When you have a highly skilled team you choose to adapt your leadership approach in order to ensure you receive their input. This contrasts with a circumstance where the team is particularly novice or lacking in the information that you hold in your leadership role.

A third variable centers on the nature of the organizational culture. Some organizations, for example, are more autocratic in nature and so a more democratic decision-making process, while preferable in my view, might be greeted with a jaundiced eye. And then the final variable influencing the strategy used for the leadership style you choose centers on the larger societal culture. In some societal cultures the capacity to engage team members in decision making may be hampered by the way in which the societal culture views leaders. For example, when I teach leadership courses to international students from China it is very difficult to get them to engage in questions during a lecture. When this first occurred, I wondered what was happening but soon realized that the students came from a region in China that considered questioning professors to be very disrespectful.

The four basic strategies should be also thought of as existing on a continuum, with the more autocratic "Tell" on one end and the more democratic "Join" on the opposite end. In between the two, I include "Sell" and "Consult." The appropriateness of using one strategy over the other is determined by the variable at play. The first strategy on the continuum, *Tell*, is the one you would use when something needs to get done quickly and when the leader/manager has knowledge that the team does not. For example, think about a brand-new team that is just forming. In these instances, the leader typically is engaged in more Tell behavior. Also, this approach is clearly used in emergencies: "No time to discuss this, there is a fire! Get out of the building and call the fire department!" Communication within the Tell mode is generally one-way in nature.

The second strategy is to *Sell*. In this instance the leader has more information than the team and feels strongly that a particular path forward is the best one. In the Sell mode the leader holds onto the decision-making authority but also wants to have some give and take with the team so that team members can fully understand the importance of pursuing the path forward identified by the leader. This involves more two-way communication than Tell and is used primarily by the leader to fully inform the team.

In my own leadership practice, I have used the Sell mode to help my team understand the importance of a particular path. For example, a decision to move into a new service for my nonprofit, one that is outside of our traditional operations, is a time when using a Sell approach is especially important. Now, to be clear, unlike the proverbial used-car sales pitch, in which the goods being sold are questionable, the Sell mode should be more akin to the servant leadership characteristic of using persuasion to help bring people on board.

There are a few important considerations in using the Sell mode. First, as noted above, you must honestly believe in what you are selling. You are better off if you simply tell the team if the pill is a bitter one. Trying to Sell if you do not honestly believe in what you are trying to communicate only comes across as disingenuous, and leadership that is perceived as anything less than genuine will be ineffective in the long run. The other consideration is that moving into the Sell mode requires more time than the Tell method. To go back to our example of a fire in the building, you would not have time to sell people on the idea of exiting the building, they simply must be told to get out!

The third strategy is to *Consult*. In the Consult mode the leader holds onto the decision-making authority but relies on the expertise of the team in order to choose the best path forward. As you would imagine, the team in this instance is skilled and holds knowledge, information, and expertise that will help inform the leader in making the best decision possible. In the Consult mode there is considerable exchange of information and communication is two-way in nature.

The leader actively works with the team to understand the ramifications of any decision that is being considered and the team is actively engaged with the leader in determining the way forward. It follows that being in the Consult mode requires considerably more time than the Tell or Sell mode.

The final strategy, representing the far end of the continuum, is the *Join* mode. In this instance the leader has presented the situation to the team and has given the team full rein to decide how to move forward. In this case the team has extensive knowledge and capabilities, and the leader is confident that their expertise makes it possible for them to pass on the decision-making authority. Now, when you are in the Join mode, you'll see that this approach takes the most time of the four identified. In addition, as a leader, you must be prepared to live with the decision that the group comes up with. If you decide to use a Join strategy, but later change your mind because you do not like the way things are going, you will find that you have damaged your team's respect for your leadership ability. Be sure to be clear when you choose this strategy.

In fact, being clear about the strategy you choose is especially important. I generally work with my leadership team in a way that helps them to understand which mode I am pursuing on the front end. For example, I will say that I have to make a decision and I very much need their input before making a final decision. This way, the team will know what to expect. If you are not clear up-front and the team feels that you have changed the strategy you've chosen midstream, your work relationship will suffer.

It is also important, in keeping with our leadership practice perspective of *awareness*, to understand that each of us has a propensity for one of these strategies over another. Some of us are comfortable with telling folks what to do. Others have a real problem in this area and prefer to join with their team members. And while you are more comfortable with one approach over another it is important to recognize that the variable in play may require that you step out of your comfort zone. Effective leadership within this context is leadership that has the capacity to move between each of the four strategies depending on the demands present.

When I was an early teen, before I received my license to drive, I used to take my grandfather's Nash Rambler out for a ride (when Grandpa was not home). My little brother would sit next to me, his head not even over the dashboard. The Rambler was a standard, gears on the column, only it did not have second gear. To get out of the driveway and up the hill to freedom I would have to gun it, first pushing the RPMs almost into the red and then throwing it into third gear. Thud, thud, thud, da, da, dut, dut, dut, the old Rambler would struggle and then with luck the third gear would take hold and we would be off and running. More times than not the old hill would make it impossible to reach third gear and we would stall out.

So, what does this have to do with choosing leadership style? A leader who does not have the ability to move successfully between the Tell, Sell, Consult, and Join modes based on the variables present is a leader who risks stalling out. Do not end up being like my granddad's old Nash Rambler. Work to raise your own self-awareness and then strive to develop your skills in any of the modes that the circumstance dictates. Do not be caught metaphorically without second gear.

Figure 3.1 provides a schema for understanding the relationship between the variable that are present and the four leadership strategies. The x-axis represents the leadership style strategies. The y-axis reflects the time involved as well as the expertise on the part of the manager or the team. As you can see, in the Tell mode, the leader exercises the most authority and has the greatest amount of information manifest as skills and abilities. As you move along the x-axis to Sell, Consult, and Join you will note that the amount of time necessary increases, as does the level of skill and ability present within the team.

Surrounding the schema is the organizational as well as the larger cultural context. These elements play an important role as well in whether the leader might pursue any of the leadership strategies identified. For example, if you happen to work in a nonprofit that is unionized, then you will have to consider the influence that this has on your decision to engage in one of the leadership strategies. Or, if you are a nonprofit that is in its early stages of development, this

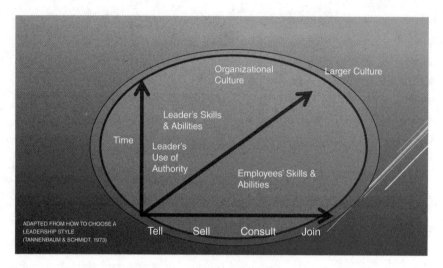

Figure 3.1   Factors Impacting Leadership Style

Source: Adapted from Tannenbaum and Schmidt (1973).

will become a consideration when you choose a successful leadership strategy. There are innumerable factors within the organization's culture as well as the larger societal culture that will play a role in how you determine which of the strategies you use.

I should also note that there is a dynamic element to using this conceptual frame. Your team, for example, is not static. New members come and go. Existing team members develop and learn new skills. As a result, you will want to develop your leadership strategy accordingly. A team that is just forming, for example, typically needs more support in the form of Tell and Sell modes to gain their footing. As they develop, you will need to transition into a Consult role and consider the Join mode as well, when appropriate.

In this chapter I have worked to frame several considerations when it comes to pursuing the development of your leadership practice. First, the notion that effective leaders should also be effective managers. The complex demands that face today's nonprofit organizations require that these two frames remain inextricably tied together. Leaders need to manage, and managers need to lead. Work to develop your practice in both areas.

In addition, we have done a 10,000-foot flyover of various leadership styles and dedicated some time to exploring servant leadership in greater detail, particularly since this approach works well within nonprofit organizations. Of course, you will want to decide which model appeals the most to you and then commit yourself to learning more about the style, knowing that you will ultimately borrow aspects from each.

We also touched on the emergent leadership models that turn their focus from thinking about leadership as the work of a single actor to strategies to enhance leadership across and throughout the organization. This is an important conceptual frame and one that we will explore in greater detail as we move through the rest of the book.

The Tannenbaum and Schmidt (1973) classic model on choosing a leadership style was also an important consideration within this chapter. This conceptual frame has been widely recognized for its ability to help leaders navigate the many variables at play as they work to advance their leadership practice. I share in the enthusiasm for this classic approach and have seen firsthand how their model can help leaders and managers to be effective.

4

Creating Positive Organizational Culture

A Well-Kept Secret

Psst, come here . . . I want to share something with you. Something that will help you advance your leadership and help your organization fulfill its mission. Now, remember the term identified earlier in this book, the word *simplexity*? Well, what we explore in this chapter is a perfect example of simplexity. More specifically we explore something that is simultaneously simple and complex. The idea is simple yet the layers that exist and the strategies to advance this important conceptual frame can be complex, while also simple—simplexity for sure.

For decades, researchers, writers, and practitioners in leadership, management, and organizational science have recognized the importance of organizational culture. Peter Drucker is attributed with saying that if you are not careful, your organization's culture will eat your strategy for breakfast. A recent Google search of the phrase "organizational culture" nets more than 190,000,000 results in less than a second. Researchers strive to understand organizational culture from all perspectives. Virgana and Kasyadi (2020), for example, studied the role that organizational culture plays in school supervisor performance. Marcos, García-Ael, and Topa (2020) studied the impact of organizational culture on the citizenship behavior of Spanish police officers. Aryani and Widodo (2020) conducted an extensive literature review to build a conceptual framework for understanding successful organizational culture. The list of studies, journal articles, and trade articles related to understanding organizational culture, for all practical purposes, is endless. The importance of developing and maintaining an effective organizational culture is widely agreed upon, yet there is a great deal of consternation about how to achieve this widely desired outcome.

What is interesting about this is the fact that all organizations have a culture in which they operate. There is no escaping this fact, yet—for a variety of reasons—we are often subject to the organization's culture rather than experiencing the opposite, which is where the organization's culture is finely tuned to support the mission and vision of the organization. There are a variety of reasons for this, and I believe one of the key reasons is that organizational culture becomes invisible to us. The social patterns and the behavior we engage in within the context of group interaction are so ingrained in us that we seldom pursue a mindful consideration of the culture that surrounds us.

A colleague and friend of mine helped me to think about the invisible nature of organizational culture with a metaphor that I feel is worth sharing. We were on a long drive, a day trip to meet with one of our nonprofit's funding sources. The drive was three and a half hours each way and we were about two and half hours into the first leg of the trip. We had been talking at length and I had just hit one of those moments when I thought it better to be quiet for a while. Perhaps you have experienced a situation like this, when I wondered if I had shared too much information with a colleague. My friend suddenly said, "I got it . . ." I turned my attention to him with a puzzled look. "No, no, I got it," he repeated. "Got what?" I asked. He turned triumphantly toward me and said, "It's like fish and water."

Now I must admit I was very perplexed and thought for a moment about simply turning my attention toward the side window to watch the highway go by, but then thought better of it. "What do you mean?" I asked. He repeated himself as if that would help me to understand. "It's like fish and water!" I was still lost. "You're going to have to help me." "Look, Paul, our organization's culture is like the water we swim in." Wow, I thought, this is out of the blue, but once I understood what he was saying, I thought the metaphor was quite profound.

Let us play with this metaphor for just a little bit; what do you think fish think about water? I suspect they do not think at all about water, unless you've got one on your fishing line and you've managed to bring them up out of their cultural waters onto the boat. Then you see a great deal of thought on their part about water, or, in this instance, the lack of water! Like fish, we swim in the cultural waters of our respective organizations. Because the culture that surrounds us is all-encompassing, we often find ourselves going about our day-to-day business unaware of how the culture is impacting us. To extend my friend's metaphor another step, it might be that the cultural waters we swim in are polluted or unhealthy for us. Because the water surrounds us, we do not stop to consider it. In fact, for reasons that we explore in this chapter, we find that we are sometimes complicit with the unhealthy waters. Think of the advantage that you will realize by helping to ensure that the cultural waters that you and your team swim in are clear, clean, and healthy.

As you work to advance your leadership capacity, you will want to develop the ability to leverage your organization's culture in a way that will help your nonprofit realize its mission and in a way that will make you and your teammates' leadership practice as successful as possible. We know from the practice perspectives discussed earlier in this book that leveraging your organization's culture will require knowing when to move in an antigravitational way, to develop your understanding of how to deal with inner pressures that may be present as well as heightening your awareness about the culture that exists and then leveraging this knowledge to pursue the culture that you desire.

In this chapter I will walk you through several important concepts as well as strategies that have proven to be extremely helpful in building and sustaining a positive organizational culture. The importance of building the right culture, one that can work to support your organization as well as your leadership capacity, cannot be overstated. Having the right culture means that you will have the bandwidth to advance your organization's mission, even in the face of significant challenges such as the COVID-19 pandemic. A rising tide lifts all boats! Having a positive culture makes it possible to improve everyone's ability to pursue their work in support of the organization's mission.

Understanding Organizational Culture

Let us agree to explore the basic elements of organizational culture and why culture takes root within the team and within the agency. First, let us start with a simple definition. An organization's culture is built from the beliefs, values, norms, rituals, and patterns of behavior developed over time as members of the organization work to adapt to both internal and external challenges that confront the group. Or said another way, it is the "way things are done around here" (Deal & Kennedy, 1982, 2000).

The power of an organization's culture to engender action and to shape the way people think and feel is significant. At the root of this is the notion that people are social beings. As such, we desire and gravitate toward belonging and membership. The membership we seek might be in formal groups, such as political parties, fraternal organizations, sports teams, professional associations, and the like, or the membership we pursue can be in informal groups, such as a social event, community groups, friends, and family. In both instances group membership informs our attitudes, our values, beliefs, and behavior.

Our need to belong drives us toward the patterns of engagement found within the group. To connect and to belong we behave as other group members behave. Consider the Girl Scouts, for example. As a formal group the Girl Scouts have a shared set of attitudes, values, beliefs, and behaviors that are taken on by those that join. They have a pledge, uniforms, rituals, and symbols in the form of badges that represent their core beliefs and signify achievement on the part of the group member. You might also choose the Hell's Angels as a formal group to explore. They also have a shared set of attitudes, values, beliefs, and behaviors. Do they have uniforms? Yes. Rituals and symbols? Yes indeed, in the form of rites of passage and colors. Each group represents a particular culture and has many similar features as the other, yet one group compared with another could be identified as a more positive force in the larger society.

So what? Well, it is important to recognize that whenever a group of people join together a specific culture will develop, and sometimes the culture's presence is positive while other times it can be a negative force within the societal frame. Herein lies our challenge. Culture happens, but the key is to learn how to create a positive culture, one that will at once serve our need as humans to be socially connected while supporting the essential work of your nonprofit organization.

The first step is to recognize the importance of leveraging our very human desire to belong by creating a positive and prosocial group that is meaningful and one that has multiple opportunities for individuals to belong. Once you accomplish this, then you will see that members will take on the attitudes, values, beliefs, and behaviors that are associated with as well as distinctly represent the group. Achieving this requires that you understand the simplexity that is present. The notion of creating a positive group that is meaningful for members with multiple opportunities to belong—resulting in members taking on the attitudes, values, beliefs, and behaviors—seems quite simple. Yet it is simultaneously quite complex.

For example, what is meaningful to one person may in fact be meaningless to another person. We also might have different opinions about what values the group can agree on as positive. In addition, we may not understand how to create meaningful opportunities for belonging. This complexity, though, should not stop us, but rather simply inform the process as we work to build a strong organizational culture.

When I train groups on how to develop a positive organizational culture, I often start with an example that highlights the complexity involved as well as some of the strategies that one can use to break down challenges and turn them into opportunities. I ask the audience to imagine that I am going to start a weekly group for music appreciation. The group will run for four hours, and I tell them that the focus will be solely on heavy metal, and we'll play it as loud as the music system will allow us. I then ask for a show of hands from those who wish to join the group. Typically, if I am lucky, one or two people in an audience of 100 will raise their hands. Then I change my approach. "Okay, we'll listen to a variety of different types of music, and then we'll set aside time to discuss what we heard and what we thought of the various musical genres." Now when I ask for a show of hands to see who is in, the number rises from 2 to 25 of 100 people from the audience. "Okay, let's try this," I announce. "Let's make sure that we have some great food available." Now I have more than half the group raising their hands. "Who can bake?" I ask. A few people show their hands and agree to help me prepare the food for the weekly event. "Who can help me choose the playlist?" I ask. Now, not only do I have a growing number of participants, but I also have a team that is helping me to pull it off, each contributing in a way that is meaningful to them. Some bakers do not particularly care for group activities, but they care about baking. Some participants do not truly care about music, but they love to eat. Others are going to come because they want to support their friends who are helping to put the event together.

The example here, while quite simple, illustrates the nuances of building a group that is meaningful and has multiple opportunities for belonging. In the first instance we had only two participants. At that point one strategy that we might have tried would be to simply mandate that everyone come. We might get a few more participants, but in the end, we would be sure to fail. Instead, we began a process of expanding participation by connecting to the participants' interests and then engaging them in the action that would ultimately result in a positive group experience. Even those who did not really care for the musical element of the group got involved!

This example can be instructive in our effort to build a positive organizational culture. The key is to be thoughtful about the various activities you engage in and the way in which you build opportunities for participation, and this chapter will assist in this effort.

The Role of Mission, Values, and Vision

The first strategy is to engage in practices that will ensure you can align the attitudes, values, beliefs, and behaviors that you desire within your organizational culture. Let us start with the importance of establishing a mission statement that is operationalized throughout your organization and your team. The mission statement serves as the foundation for all that you do within your organization. Everything that you engage in, every strategy that you pursue, and the way in which you and your team work together should rest firmly on the mission statement. Consider the picture of the foundation here as a metaphor for your mission statement. The mission statement must be well grounded and firmly constructed. Your services, the systems you use, and your organizational structure must be built firmly on top of your mission statement. As you look at the picture shown here, imagine that this is your future home and your contractor just came to you and said that he wanted to add a new kitchen and that he thought, since you had room in the yard, that it would make sense to build the kitchen in the dirt right next to the house. I imagine you would very quickly fire the contractor and find someone new. A kitchen with a $60,000 price tag built in the dirt? That contractor is out of his mind.

While I am sure you agree, I do want to say that I have many times seen a nonprofit organization that either has not taken the time to build and maintain a strong mission or, equally as concerning, they have a strong mission that serves as their foundation, but have built their services, systems, and structures separately, as if off in a random dirt lot. Anything that you build and develop outside of the foundation of your mission is bound to fail and can also pull down the rest of the house.

The Organization's Mission is like a Strong Foundation

From my practice I have found that the best mission statement for any nonprofit organization is a simple statement, one that is clear and one that everyone can agree to as the premise for your organization's purpose. When I think about effective mission statements I also think about the notion of sugaring. If you are from the New England area, you are likely familiar with the term *sugaring*. Simply stated, sugaring is the process of making syrup from the sap of maple trees. Now there are long-held debates about which of the northern New England States make the best syrup—some say Vermont, others New Hampshire, and still others say Maine. There is also an ongoing argument about the ratio of sap to syrup. Some say 40 gallons of sap to one gallon of syrup, some say 30 gallons of sap. Arguments aside, the reason that I think about sugaring when it comes to mission statements is the idea that many nonprofit organizations build mission statements that are, to be honest, a lot of sap. They have not taken the time to carefully craft a mission statement that people can agree upon, that can be easily remembered and easily integrated as an important reference point throughout the organization's day-to-day operations. Remember, it is essential that your mission statement serve as the foundation for everything you do and mission statements that are sap-based typically live on the wall or in a policy folder, are dangerously disconnected from the day-to-day work of the organization, and as a result are not fully operationalized.

By contrast, when a nonprofit organization has taken the time to develop a carefully crafted, grade A (short and sweet) mission statement, they find that they are better prepared to integrate their fundamental purpose into the day-to-day work being pursued. They are less likely to stray from the foundation that serves as a key starting point for defining their purpose, as well as the things that the organization holds near and dear. The mission statement, done well, provides the organization with firm footing for what the agency believes to be important and what is valued above all.

Where I serve as the executive director, we worked together to develop a mission statement that is boiled down to the essentials upon which we can all agree. Our mission is to *inspire and empower people so that they can reach their full potential and live successfully within their own home and community*. This mission provides the foundation for everything we do. We repeatedly ask ourselves if we are working effectively, for example, to empower the people we serve. We examine how our array of services fulfills our desire to help people to reach their full potential and live in their own community. Are the new programming and service delivery options that present themselves perfectly aligned with our mission or should we shy away because pursuing the course of action would be like building the proverbial kitchen in the dirt? This type of ongoing assessment is part and parcel with understanding whether we are living our mission statement. Having a clear and well-thought-out mission statement is critical to your ability to begin the process of building a strong organizational culture.

Hand in glove with a strong mission statement are the values and beliefs that inform your organization's practice. Developing a list of clearly articulated and actualized value and belief statements becomes an important way to consider whether the team and the organization are truly fulfilling the agency's mission statement. The values you subscribe to have to go beyond those listed on a website or in a policy book. The values and beliefs must be seen in how the team works with each other and how the team works with the people the organization serves. In my nonprofit organization we focus on and strive to actualize values focused around respect and empowerment for all, participant-driven service delivery, embracing diversity, supporting individual talents and the needs of all people, and striving to always learn and grow together. Your organization's values and beliefs may have some similarities or may be altogether different. What is important is that the values and beliefs are articulated by the team as well as seen in the day-to-day work of the organization. The key is to have clearly articulated values and beliefs that are easily seen in the actions taken by all members of the organization.

It is important that the values and beliefs your organization subscribes to cut across the organization no matter your title or role. The business office or the corporate office, for example, should engage in their work in a way that reflects the values and beliefs held dear to the organization's pursuit of its mission. Do not fall into the trap of having a different standard for those who receive services from the organization and the individuals who provide services, when it comes to these critical values and beliefs. To build a strong culture you must work to ensure that the efforts to pursue the mission and actualize the shared beliefs and values are pursued across the entire organization.

It is especially important to recognize the adverse impact that comes to the organization's culture if any of the team members do not say what they do and do what they say. If we speak the values and beliefs but do not behave in that way, we do a disservice to the desire to create a positive organizational culture. Congruence is critical and any part of the organization or team that holds itself to a separate standard will ultimately become a fault line in your effort to build a strong organization culture.

I have seen this firsthand and know the impact incongruence can have on the organization. I mentioned the business office as an example; in my work with organizations to build a positive organizational culture I have seen nonprofit business offices of an organization behave as if they believed they would have a great business office if it were not for all these annoying services and program staff! As soon as you have a department or level of the organization with this attitudinal stance you have a serious problem on your hands.

Congruence across the organization about values and beliefs in line with the agency's mission will help buttress you against challenges of this nature.

A clearly articulated vision, when combined with your operationalized mission, values, and beliefs, provides a potent context for pursuing a positive organizational culture. Morden (1997) defines vision as "an imagined or perceived but consistent pattern of communal possibilities to which others can be drawn, and whose values they wish to share." When leadership provides a clear and well-articulated vision for the team or the organization there is a call to action that includes the capacity to think about how we would like things to be—a desired state, if you will. A clearly articulated vision also helps to clarify values and beliefs. Actively pursuing a vision for the team or the organization helps to separate the "wheat from the chaff." Some team members will quickly embrace the vision and associated values while others will not. When the organization's values and beliefs are fully actualized, individuals who disagree with the vision will either rework their own beliefs and get on board or choose to get off at the next stop. And while we do not like to lose team members, it is better to have those who disagree with the organization's fundamental values and beliefs go somewhere else to work rather than have them continue with their negative contribution to the organization's efforts.

There are several techniques for capitalizing on the use of the organization's vision. As a leader it is important to share your vision for the organization and work with your team to talk about and build a shared vision for the agency's future. You can also build vision development and pursuit into your strategic planning processes. An approach for pursuing vision through strategic planning is explored in Chapter 8.

The Power of Norms

Up to this point I have written about the importance of a clearly identified strong mission statement and lived values and beliefs, along with a well-articulated vision for the organization. Care should be taken to ensure that each of these elements is in place and, as you pursue an organizational culture that has a shared mission, values, beliefs, and vision, it is important to take some time to examine some of the fundamental elements of group and organizational culture.

Let's start with a few terms that can help us to understand the organization's or group's culture. First it is important to consider the power of group norms and the role that norms play in how we engage in group and organizational life. Norms, simply defined, are, in the purest sense, *unspoken expectations that govern our behavior based on group membership.* When norms take hold there's no need to talk about how people will or should behave. The individual, as they join the group, begins to take on the unspoken expectations that govern their behavior based on their membership. As we noted earlier, the Girl Scouts have a wide array of norms that are aligned with how the group behaves; biker gangs as well are subject to group norms.

If you are reading this book as a part of a course, then you can quickly consider the types of norms that exist in your class. Hopefully, you will see a positive norm that is manifest in the way that your classmates talk one at a time and are willing to listen to other points of view, perhaps even raising their hand (in person or in a Zoom class) before they speak. My guess is, taking it to the absurd, that they arrive in class dressed in clothing, wearing socks and shoes, and not in their pajamas (although the advent of virtual and telelearning has shaken this norm up!). I doubt that your professor had to send people home to get dressed before class started. If you are reading this book on the commuter train or sitting in your office, you, too, are surrounded by norms—norms that are created as a result of your membership in a given group or culture. Norms, as unspoken expectations that govern behavior, are a powerful force within groups and play an important role in the nature of the culture that exists within your organization.

Norms can be positive in that they help to uphold the organization's mission, vision, values, and beliefs by supporting behavior that is congruent with the organization's efforts or they can be a negative force detracting from the ability to realize the same. I recall one of many examples I have observed in which a group norm adversely impacted a nonprofit organization that I was working with. I was asked to help them with their team's communication practices, as they were experiencing quite a bit of discord between team members. The team was not dealing with each other directly and there seemed to be a lack of buy-in across the organization.

As I sat in the initial planning meeting with the 12 managers, I quickly noticed that team members began one at a time to look at their smartphone. This was not just one or two managers; everyone seemed to take a turn at one point or another. Soon I noticed that one manager was sending a text and then to my surprise one of the managers from across the table began to respond to the manager who sent the text. Somehow this group had developed a norm that said, checking your phone is fine, and if you want to send a private message to someone else in the meeting, go for it! Now the irony of why I was there was not lost on me and so I politely interrupted the executive director to ask if I could share my observation with the group and how it seemed connected to my purpose for joining them.

Because our norms are so powerful and because they can cut both ways by being either a positive or a negative force in your desire to build your organizational or group culture, it is important to think about strategies for supporting the right kind of norms within your organization. Feldman (1984) provides a classic yet important frame for considering why norms exist and how norms can be shaped to support the work of the organization. Feldman posits that norms take hold for two basic reasons. First, they exist in order to achieve something in a group setting. To get something done! Imagine working as a group and being in the situation where there were no norms at all. Consider the example offered earlier of taking a course and being in class. Without norms there would be complete chaos. People would talk all at once, not know enough to sit at a desk; some would come still dressed in their PJs, and others would not even know enough to show up to class! Norms are developed to ensure the presence of group processes and behaviors that will support the desired goal.

The second reason for norms to take hold within a culture is our inherent desire to feel comfortable in a group setting. We are, in the words of the great bluesman Howlin' Wolf, "built for comfort." In social situations we naturally gravitate toward behavior and actions that help us to feel comfortable. As we have discussed, we want to belong and we want to feel a part of the group. We also like to know what to expect and we want things to go smoothly. This desire for comfort and predictability is extremely powerful and is a force that is present throughout all our social interactions. For example, can you think of a time when you arrived at a social event of some type and your clothing was not consistent with the rest of the attendees? You are stuck there, and you have to simply live through it.

I recall once being called to a Friday meeting on the spur of the moment by the executive director of the local United Way. That very same morning I had sat staring in my bureau drawer at home considering what to wear for "dress-down day." I distinctly recall choosing one of the rattiest pairs of jeans that I owned. I thought, *I'm not going anywhere today, just the office, it will be okay.* When I received the call, I explained to the United Way executive director that I was not really dressed for an official meeting. She said, "Don't worry, it's just one or two of us." I will never forget the feeling when the elevator doors opened onto the glass-walled conference room at the top of the hospital complex and there—to my surprise—along with the executive director of the United Way sat the state Speaker of the House and the President of the Senate. Those ratty old blue jeans caused me a lot of embarrassment during a very uncomfortable meeting.

"So what?" you ask, "Who cares?" Why do we care why norms take hold? Well, if we can agree that norms take hold to get something done, then it is critical that you communicate with your team, your group, and your organization what it is that you hope to get done. Shared goals become an important part of the formula for supporting the norms that you desire.

Years ago, when I ran a community residence for young adults who had been institutionalized for many years in the state psychiatric hospital, my team and I found ourselves battling innumerable negative norms, norms that had their genesis in the back wards of the state hospital system. I remember that my team was becoming weary and was beginning to question our ability to help the young adults transition successfully into the community. We had tried every way possible to build strong positive norms within our residence but seemed to get stymied at every turn.

At a staff meeting we were talking about what to do. I sat quietly and then said, "I know, we'll build a softball team." The look I received from my team members was a combination of shock and what I perceived to be wondering on their part about looking for another job! I think they felt their leader had lost his mind. I said it again, more affirmatively. "We'll build a softball team." Now up until this point we had been trying to build positive norms, but we had not really pulled together clear goals that the entire community could buy into. To build a team we needed uniforms, we had to have a team manager, do fundraising, reach out to other community residences to build a schedule, and practice. As we discussed earlier, we quickly found something *meaningful* for every member of the community, and our desire to get this done gave us the ability to build positive norms.

As a result, we built our softball team. Everyone rallied and became involved in the various activities. The young adults within the program became invested in the effort and everyone played their part. Interestingly enough, more mental health services were delivered as a result of people having something meaningful to engage in than would have happened if we simply kept hitting our head against the proverbial wall without establishing meaningful goals that the group could coalesce around.

Since norms also take hold because of our desire to be comfortable and have predictability in a group, it is important to understand that the presence of positive norms within your group will play an important role in helping new members take on the positive behaviors associated with the group's positive norms. When you become a part of the group and you encounter norms that are inconsistent with what you believe, then you are said to be in a state of *cognitive dissonance* (see, for example, Schacter & Gazzaniga, 1990). This occurs when your thoughts and your feelings are not aligned with your behavior. Cognitive dissonance is extremely uncomfortable and, do not forget, we are built for comfort. The story of my rattiest jeans serves as an example of a time when I experienced cognitive dissonance. My behavior, in terms of my clothing, was not aligned with my thoughts and feelings. I thought, based on who was in the room, that I should have been better dressed—and I felt terrible as a result—yet I sat there in the glass conference room at a glass conference table with my raggedy jeans on.

When you or a team member are in a state of cognitive dissonance, there are potentially two ways to resolve the discomfort: (1) you change your behavior to align with your thoughts and feelings or (2) you change your thoughts and feelings. In both instances the outcome is that the discomfort caused by the cognitive dissonance is resolved. Trust me, in the example shared I decided to no longer wear my most worn-out jeans on dress-down day, and I resolved to no longer accept invites from the executive director of the United Way to any "small meetings" on Fridays.

Taken together, these two powerful reasons for the omnipresence of norms in group settings provide you with a window for considering the role that norms can play in creating a positive organizational culture. Now, take the two reasons for the presence of norms—to get things done and for comfort in social settings—and marry this with our desire to belong and the work that you are doing to actualize your mission, vision, values, and beliefs, and you will have a strong formula for building team and group behavior that supports a positive organizational culture.

We know that norms form as we work in social settings to get something done. We also know that our desire to be comfortable in social settings helps us to work through cognitive dissonance to achieve a sense of balance and congruence. And we can use this knowledge to help integrate new members into the positive norms that exist. But what about those of us who are suffering from negative norms that are adversely impacting our ability to build a strong organizational culture, pursue the organization's vision, and realize the agency's mission? Feldman's (1984) classic work along with my own baptism-by-fire experience has helped to develop a response to this question that will support your efforts to change negative norms within your team and your organization.

There are five factors that inform strategies to build the type of norms that will help create a positive organizational culture. As we explore the five factors, I want you to think of each one as an important part of a recipe for shaping the desired norms within your culture. As with any recipe, it is important to consider the role that each ingredient plays as well as the fact that each ingredient must be proportioned properly to achieve the desired outcome. To extend this metaphor I think about baking bread and how a good bread recipe has just the right amount of oil, flour, yeast or starter dough, salt, and water. You would not take four cups of flour and put it in the oven at 450 degrees and in 40 minutes expect to have bread, would you? Of course not. In fact, you would be lucky if you did not end up with a fire on your hands. Similarly, as we explore the five factors that shape norms it is important to include all the ingredients to ensure you achieve the desired outcome.

The first factor that informs how norms, or unspoken expectations that govern behavior, are formed is the idea of *primacy*. Primacy is how things happen first. It is the first time you meet someone, the first time that you attend a training by a particular presenter, your first evaluation as an employee, first day on the job, or any number of firsts. Primacy is seen ultimately as a litany of firsts. For example, a new employee has a first day at work, and this helps to inform him or her about the norms that are within the group, office, or program location. Then this same individual will attend their first staff meeting, have their first job review with their supervisor, the first offline private conversations with coworkers. In each instance, how the individual experiences these various forms of primacy informs them about the norms that are present.

Consider a new employee who hears from human resources on their first day that the company is very interested in how their employees are experiencing their work and that the entire agency encourages questions at any step along the way. This begins to build an expectation that the norms support open dialogue. Then the employee, now at the worksite, begins to ask questions and is received by their supervisor in a favorable way: "Thanks for asking," "Let me see if I can help you," "That's a great question." Because the employee is experiencing congruence between what the human resource office has said in the employee's initial primacy and what their new supervisor says at the work site, the employee's understanding about the importance of this norm is heightened and they are more likely to participate and support an environment that welcomes open dialogue and questions.

Primacy plays an important role in how norms are shaped within the organization. It is important to not only recognize this but also to be intentional in how you manage this litany of primacy as each opportunity presents itself. For example, I think very carefully about how I can leverage primacy to help support the norms that I desire within the organization. When I meet someone new on the team, I am aware of the impact of how I engage with them and the role that it plays in creating the type of norms that are desired within the organization. If someone comes to me for the first time with a problem, the manner in which I respond plays an important role in the norms that will be established going forward. Do not give it away! Be thoughtful about this idea of primacy and leverage it whenever you are able to help build positive norms within the organization.

Another factor that contributes to the way norms are formed within the group is the use of spoken expectations. When we talk together about how we would like the norms to be within the organization, we are able to help set the course for future patterns of behavior. Spoken expectations about desired norms make it possible to help group members clarify what is important to the team as well as establish some guidelines that will help the team be successful. Of course, there must be congruence between the spoken expectations that you share and the behavior that you portray, and what is seen within the group. You can say, "Around here we're all respectful and listen to each other" as much as you want, but if you or your team is behaving counter to this, the spoken expectation will not carry much weight.

Returning to our bread metaphor I often think about the norm-shaping factor of spoken expectations as akin to the flour in the recipe. It is often the most visible part of the recipe and is generally seen in great quantity. But as noted earlier, four cups of flour in a bread pan is not bread: it's just flour. Given this, it is important to clearly talk about what we expect for our team's and organization's norms, and to be sure to include the other ingredients.

The third factor that shapes norms is found in the impact of significant events. Significant events play an important role in how norms are shaped within the organization's culture. When I present to a large group on this topic, I always ask the audience to raise their hand if they can think of a significant event that has shaped norms. Up until March 2020 participants would inevitably raise their hand and say "9/11." This was the response 100 percent of the time. Since March 2020, the answer has changed, and I am sure you've guessed why. Now participants say that the COVID-19 pandemic has significantly impacted norms.

Both responses are valid; each significant event has shaped the norms within the larger culture in many ways. Think about what it was like to travel pre-9/11 and what it is like to travel now. Pre-9/11, Mrs. Dann would walk with me to my gate at the airport and give me a kiss goodbye as I jumped on the flight with 10 minutes to spare. Try to do that today! Similarly, the pandemic has changed the way we interact, how we travel, how we work, and how we play. Significant events shape norms!

Now, it is important to recognize that the two significant events we just recognized are both traumatic and negative experiences that many would argue have adversely impacted our societal norms. Recall that our goal is to build positive norms that will support the growth and presence of a positive organizational culture. For this reason, I am calling on you to use what we know about the power of significant events to create positive experiences that will help support the positive norms you desire. A significant event can be an impressive activity that everyone comes away from saying "Wow! That was awesome!" or it can be something as simple as a small but impactful moment with only a few people. Either can have the power to shape the norms within your company's culture.

For example, in my nonprofit organization we have an annual conference in which we engage in team building, professional development, and the celebration of our work. This conference has become a significant event in and of itself. Employees help provide the training, team members who did not get to go this year hope to go the following year, and the opportunity to connect builds a sense of belonging and community within the context of our work and the agency's mission. During this event we also give out employee awards in five categories. Each of the categories underscores core values and beliefs found within the organization. Courage to Grow, Superhero Award, and the Shining Star Award are three of the categories, and as you can imagine from the titles of the awards, they each show the importance of agency-held values. Individuals who receive the Courage to Grow are employees who have taken strides to develop themselves. Superheroes have gone above and beyond, and Shining Stars are superb role models. Individuals who receive these awards as well as those who witness the awards being presented are being impacted by a significant event, which in turn is helping to shape positive norms.

Now a less grand, yet equally important example of a positive significant event could be seen in something as simple as how an employee's annual evaluation is conducted. If the evaluation is fair and the content is something that the employee is aware of and something that they are working on, and if the process is one that is supportive, in which the supervisor and the supervisee are fully engaged, then this can be seen as a significant event as well. The key here is that significant events are defined by the individual who is experiencing the event as important to them. In this light a significant event can be something as simple as a phone call from the leader to check in on how a team member is doing after a difficult day or it can be something as grand as the aforementioned conference or employee awards.

As a leader, be thoughtful about how you work to ensure that there are significant events occurring to support the desired norms within the organization. There have been many instances in my career when I've seen organizations simply ignore the power they have to shape norms by creating events that will be defined by participants as significant. Instead, they take an approach that is akin to a once-prevalent bumper-sticker slogan: "Shit happens." Now I can guarantee you that if you sit back and watch, negative significant events *will occur*. It's better to get ahead of the events that create negative norms by intentionally working to create positive significant events, which in turn leverages your ability to create positive norms. Be proactive and you will see the benefit of using this factor to shape your team's norms.

The fourth factor that shapes norms is the previous experiences held by individual group members. We have all been in other group situations and so when we come to a new group situation, we bring with us the norms that existed in the earlier group experience. This actually can be quite helpful and is the reason why students in my graduate classes at the university are able to quickly take their seats when they enter the classroom. For the same reason when you enter a conference room for a meeting you know where to sit or know that you should raise your hand to make a comment in a training or seminar. Previous experiences help us to quickly work together in a group setting toward shared goals as well as help to hit that sweet spot of comfort within a new group setting.

There is a dark side, however, to the way that previous experiences influence the group's norms. Sometimes the norms established in earlier group settings are negative norms and can adversely impact your ability to build and support your group's positive norms. One example is what I call the BBE, the bad boss experience. I imagine most of you have had a BBE before. Imagine that you have had a BBE and now find yourself with a new boss, who says, "Around here we all work together as a team and support each other." That's exactly what your previous boss said before stabbing you in the back and throwing you to the wolves, so when you hear that sentence, what you think internally is perceived as *Warning, warning!*

As a leader it is critically important to understand that new group members bring their previous experiences with them, which can either help to buoy the positive norms of the team or can negatively impact the norms. In your role, watching for this means that you will know when to underscore something positive as well as when you need to provide some added support to avert the impact of potential negative norms. When someone brings negative baggage from a normative standpoint, the individual generally needs help learning how this new environment is different from their last environment. There is a teaching as well as an employee engagement element when it comes to working with the previous experience factor. As a leader and as a team, watch for times when the new member might need some support to understand how the norms are different with your organization, and when they are bringing new positive norms, work to ensure that these norms are supported.

The fifth ingredient for factors that shape norms within the team and organization is the history of the group. Each group develops a collective history that informs their ability to adjust, adapt, and manage the various internal and external challenges they have experienced. Over time the history of the group can either help or hinder your ability to build positive norms that will strengthen your desire for a positive organizational culture. A team that has been successful in managing many different challenges sees a challenge as something doable. They might even feel that the challenge could be an opportunity to improve their capacity to pursue their work.

However, teams that have a history of challenges that resulted in failure typically have a different view of any new challenges. Instead of seeing the challenge as an opportunity, they can see it as certain failure. I recall once stepping in to run a residential treatment program and this particular group had experienced multiple failures (their words to me at the time). The team was so downtrodden that they generally did not have a sense of hope about what they could accomplish. When the supervisor called me after hours with a problem to be dealt with he with would typically say, after some discussion about options for dealing with the situation, "Well, when that doesn't work, then what?" The comment was emblematic of exactly how this team felt and so the norms or unspoken expectations that govern behavior based on group membership always looked at the glass as half empty.

When the history of the group is a largely positive one, it makes sense as a leader to be sure to share stories about the team's successes, to reflect on all that has been accomplished, and regularly remind the team of what they are capable of. For teams that have a history that includes more negative norms, it makes sense to work at reframing their history. I use an appreciative approach in which I underscore what was done well, even if it did not result in the desired end. The other strategy that goes along with this reframing effort is the importance of talking about the vision and helping people on the team talk about their desired state. How do we want to be as a team and how will we know when we have arrived at that point? What will things look like and how will it be different? Helping people to reframe their experience from an appreciative standpoint while they consider a future desired state helps the team members let go of earlier negative norms.

The five factors—primacy, spoken expectations, significant events, previous experiences, and the history of the group—provide a potent backdrop for developing strategies that help ensure the creation of positive norms within your team and organization. Using the recipe metaphor, it is important to consider how to have the right amount of each ingredient in your efforts to build positive norms and how each ingredient interacts with the others. For example, a positive primacy experience can be felt as a significant event by a new team member and can help address negative norms from previous experiences. The factors are not mutually exclusive and when strategies to leverage the factors are thoughtfully developed each contributes in its own way to the development of positive group norms.

As an example, I recall when my nonprofit was awarded a large contract to take on six transitional housing community residences that had been up and running with another provider for more than 15 years. We had four weeks to hire 60 staff and the plan, as given to us by the funding source, was to take on the operations at the stroke of midnight on New Year's Eve. We were fortunate enough to find 20 excellent staff from the existing team but had only managed to hire and train an additional 20 staff, leaving us with 20 vacancies. As a result, we pulled 20 employees from the rest of the organization who volunteered to work along with the 20 employees from the previous organization and the 20 new employees.

Our entire management team was on site at 10 p.m. on New Year's Eve and we accepted the keys at the stroke of midnight. Once I had a sense that things were going along as planned, I headed home around 2 a.m. and then returned the next day to see how things were going and if there was anything I could do to help. As I walked around and checked into each residence I asked if there was anything anyone needed. At the first residence the staff recognized me as the executive director of the agency and I suspect that this is the reason they politely said "Thank you, but we are all set." At the second residence I encountered one of the supervisors and asked her what I could do. She looked at me for a moment and said, "Well, you could go over to the pharmacy and pick up some prescriptions." I was thrilled to have something helpful to do so I jumped at the opportunity and went off to the pharmacy to pick up the prescriptions. Later I heard that she was dumbfounded that she had just sent the executive director on an errand.

Given this example it is fair to ask what norm-shaping factors were in play and what norms were impacted. First, taking on the project was clearly a significant event, not only for the organization but also for all the team members involved. Because we recognized the importance of this, we used an all-hands-on-deck approach, even at midnight on New Year's Eve. Not only were we building norms due to the significant nature of this undertaking, norms that underscored how everyone in this organization helped, but we were also exposing the new staff as well as the staff who had worked with the previous provider to a strong dose of positive primacy. The supervisor who sent me to the pharmacy, for example, who had worked with the earlier provider, shared how much it meant to work for an organization where even the executive director came out to assist.

Previous experiences were also coming into play. Many employees who had worked for the previous organization could not get over the fact that employees from other services came from as far as four hours away to volunteer their time and that leaders and managers from our organization were readily accessible and involved—"Wow, people really care around here." The employees who volunteered to help also shared their previous experiences with their program's start-up and how the agency worked to support their employees. This combined with spoken expectations along with the history of the group helped to support the development and implementation of positive norms as we worked together to achieve a significant goal.

Taken together, it's extremely important to develop your awareness of the norms that exist within your team and to consider what norms you wish to support and what the norms are that you would like to pursue. The five factors help you to think about strategies to pursue norm development and the effort to shape norms should be built firmly on the organization's mission, be aligned with the vision, and be manifest in a way that underscore the values, beliefs, and desired behaviors of the organization.

We know that agencies that possess a strong positive organizational culture are better at almost everything than agencies without one. They are more adaptive, more responsive, better able to deliver high-quality services, and can meet challenges and achieve goals and objectives. A positive organizational culture helps everyone to succeed. Employees who might otherwise be marginal find that they can succeed, learn, and grow. Donors and funders are also more attracted to organizations with positive culture.

You might even argue that, in the end, the ability to realize your organization's purpose is dependent on the nature of the organization's culture. We know this, but often leaders feel relatively powerless to advance their organization's culture to the point where this power can be harnessed. In this chapter you have been afforded some proven strategies that advance the ability to develop a positive organizational culture.

Understanding why culture takes hold and pursuing the building blocks to establish a positive culture through the use of a strong mission, vision, values, and beliefs set the stage to build and maintain strong organizational norms which in turn support the normative culture that is desired. Understanding why norms take hold and connecting this knowledge with norm-shaping strategies provides a recipe for shaping your organization's culture. Remember . . . culture happens, and it is up to you and the team to work in a way that helps to ensure that the type of organizational culture realized is the type that will ensure the success of your nonprofit organization.

5

Leadership Development in Action: The Generative Leadership Advantage

To THIS POINT we have explored several important ideas as we strive to advance a framework that will help you build your leadership practice. In earlier chapters we delved into the importance of pursuing leadership as a practice, the need to build a toolbox, and the importance of developing practice perspectives, as well as considering the type of leadership style you would like to pursue. From a lens that is more individually based, we moved into a consideration of what it takes to build a positive organizational culture—a culture that will help to ensure your nonprofit organization's capacity to realize its mission.

We turn now to another important consideration in advancing effective management and leadership practice that focuses on building strong *leadership development* capability at the individual, team, and organizational level. In this chapter we explore a leadership development frame that I call generative leadership (Dann, 2008). As you will read, *generative leadership* is a leadership development strategy that focuses on the co-creation of leadership practice within and across the organization. It is distinctive from traditional leadership development strategies because it focuses on the capacity to engender leadership behavior at the individual employee, the team, and the organizational level through *action*.

Developing leadership practice using an action-based approach moves away from the traditional focus on the positional leaders and what Rost (1993) identifies as the content of leadership. Instead, generative leadership concerns itself with a multilevel understanding of the nature of leadership development within the organization. This focus goes beyond a traditional leadership development curriculum, which is largely deterministic in nature, to consider instead the multilayered and dynamic context surrounding leadership development.

Generative leadership, in contrast to traditional leadership development activities, is centered on the *doing* rather than the *being* of leadership. Traditional leadership development models have stressed the importance of the individual leader, the characteristics they need to possess, and the skills needed to be effective (Probert & Turnbull James, 2011). By contrast, generative leadership focuses on the elements necessary to ensure that leadership capacity is present throughout the organization. The generative leadership approach makes it possible to explore the action-based side of leadership practice and leadership development in order to ensure successful leadership practice within your nonprofit organization.

The definition and use of the term *generative leadership* shouldn't be confused with Ericson's use of *generativity* (Erikson, 1993). The term as I use it here is drawn from the literal definition of each word. The word "generative" is defined as the capacity to produce while the word "leadership" is defined as the capacity to lead. Taken together "generative leadership" means the production of the capacity to lead. Simply stated, generative leadership is leadership that begets leadership. Generative leadership becomes the point of intersection between what we know to be effective leadership practice and the actions and activity necessary to yield effective leadership across and within the organization.

The importance of developing strategies to ensure that leadership is being generated throughout your nonprofit organization comes from the recognition that today's nonprofit organizations are faced with increased complexity and demand. My own nonprofit organization, for example, provides an array of services across the life continuum with an amalgam of funding sources (up to five funding sources to provide services to a single individual). This complexity means our success is dependent on the ability of our team at all levels to manage multiple tasks, responsibilities, stakeholders, and dynamics. To be successful I need my team to be fully engaged and capable of exercising leadership behavior without regard to their position within the agency.

Because of this increasing complexity there is a growing need to develop leaders who can effectively lead dynamic and complex organizational systems (Bennet & Bennet, 2004). Traditional leaders, those who are dependent on assigned roles and hierarchical structure, find themselves straining to respond to new organizational forms. There is a growing demand to consider leadership models that go beyond the visionary individual (Nadler & Tushman, 1990). In response to the changing operating environment, nonprofit organizations have increasingly evolved to meet the definition of a complex adaptive system (Pascale, 1999) and, as a result, leadership development efforts need to consider alternatives to the traditional top-down, hierarchically dependent models of leadership.

The complexity within the operating environment has set the stage for the development of new leadership paradigms. As we touched upon in Chapter 3, these paradigms work to support the development of leadership activities throughout the organization, rather than relying on the individual or individuals at the top of the organization's hierarchy. Leaderful practice and shared, cooperative, collaborative, distributive, and parallel leadership represent but a few of the models of leadership that have begun to present themselves in response to the growing complexity of both for-profit and nonprofit organizations (Andrews & Crowther, 2002; Bennet & Bennet, 2004; Pearce & Conger, 2003; Raelin, 2003; Spillane, 2006). Each brings the conceptual frame of collaboration to the leadership construct. The rise in complexity found within the nonprofit sector—complexity in consumer needs, funding mechanisms, strategic alliances, technology, and networking—have created a context that requires this movement toward collaborative models of leadership.

The conceptual frame of generative leadership comes from research I conducted on the phenomenon of action-based leadership development. In a two-year study, three leadership teams across three complex multiservice nonprofit organizations were studied using a qualitative naturalistic inquiry research design. Twenty-seven members of the respective organization's senior leader teams were interviewed using an inductive data collection model designed to build an understanding of how leadership behavior is co-created within the respective organizations. The results of the study provide an important window into strategies that I use to build successful leadership practice within nonprofit organizations. You, too, will now have the ability to not only conceptualize this model but also pursue strategies to ensure that your team and your organization's capacity for generative leadership is fully present within your agency.

Core Elements of Generative Leadership Practice

At the heart of the generative leadership model are six core elements along with seven related themes. The core elements and related subthemes are explored in some detail in this section and form the basis of an assessment tool found in the Appendix that you can use to assess the presence of generative leadership within your own organization and team. The tool makes it possible to identify areas of strength as well as areas for growth within each of the elements and related themes. The assessment tool also makes it possible to consider the presence of the core elements and related themes at three levels: the individual, the team, and at the organizational level. Scoring high at any level is indicative of that level's ability to support generative leadership practice. Lower scores provide you with a window into areas for improvement.

The core elements and related subthemes are presented in order of importance. Pursuing strategies to advance the more important elements and subthemes will help yield greater results as you work to build your own, your team's, and your organization's ability to engage in generative leadership. Building on your organization's capacity to engage in generative leadership will help to increase the presence of leadership co-creation within the organization and through this advance the agency's ability to pursue its mission and vision.

Expectations, communication and feedback, individual leadership attributes, trust, risk-taking, and opportunity are the six core elements identified through the research. The related subthemes, also weighted in order of importance via axial coding, include *having a voice, commitment, perceived need to act, organizational philosophy and practice, role modeling, shared beliefs and values,* and *structure.* The themes are interrelated and were identified through the research as playing a role in the co-creation of leadership between team members.

Each of the elements and themes is briefly described next.

Expectations

As you might have expected, the presence of expectations related to engaging in leadership practice plays the most significant role in whether employees engage in leadership behavior. If your organization desires more leadership behavior on the part of team members, it is crucial that this desire be expressed as an expectation to the entire team and throughout the organization. This can be done through spoken word, but also should be reflected in policies and practices, and be reinforced through the overall culture that is found within the team and the organization.

The importance of expectations and the role that this element plays in helping to realize desired outcomes is well documented in the literature. For example, Cangemi and Miller (2007) conducted research which showed clear expectations help employees go beyond the minimum. A team that possesses clear expectations about everyone's responsibility to engage in leadership behavior will see team members going beyond the minimum to engage in leadership behavior.

I have also seen in my own practice how expectations pay a critical role in whether team members engage in leadership behavior. I recently provided consultation to two organizations, one where the expectation to take on leadership behavior was explicit at all levels of the organization and one where the expectation was to "stay in your own lane," a euphemism for "mind your own business." The contrast between the two organizations was quite stark. The organization that expected leadership behavior on the part of team members was vibrant and highly engaged at all levels, while the organization that expected employees to mind their business was having some serious challenges adapting to the demands they encountered. Employees simply "stayed in their own lane" and the demands on the traditional hierarchical leadership were simply too much to manage.

To be clear, if you are going to ask and expect people to be engaged in leadership practice at all levels within the organization, you should be prepared to do just that! The organization with high leadership expectations is the organization that is a busy place and those with the formal leadership roles need to make room to allow for all the engagement that will come as a result of strong expectations about leadership behavior.

Communication and Feedback

Inextricably connected to the importance of clear expectations is the critical nature of communication and feedback. If the organization truly desires leadership practice across and throughout the agency, it is essential that communication and feedback occur regularly to support this desired outcome. Communication about the importance of employees taking a leadership stance should be multilayered and found not only in policies but also in regular communications, written and verbal, across the organization.

Feedback, as we discussed in the leadership practice perspectives, should be solicited, two-way, checked for accuracy, and timely. In addition, it helps to systematize as well as normalize how feedback is provided. Make sure that team members can receive feedback about their pursuit of leadership behavior regularly and be sure to engage in positive feedback. We all know that constructive feedback is helpful, but what we often forgo is ensuring that people receive on balance just slightly more positive feedback than the constructive type. Too many supervisors fall into a pattern of predominantly "constructive feedback," which in turn becomes negative.

The importance of the theme of feedback is also underscored within the literature. Lawrence and Wiswell (1993) and Smither, London, and Reilly (2005) identify how feedback helps the team to work better together and Raelin identifies feedback as providing a "reflective space" so that their inner self has time to consider the growth and self-discovery necessary to enhance their ability to lead (Raelin, 2003, p. 63).

Leadership Attributes

Another element central to the development of generative leadership practice centers on leadership attributes that include the skills and capabilities seen as inherent in the individual as well as those that were developed through experience and training. This, of course, should not come as a surprise to you as we often think about leadership attributes that are present within the individual. What is interesting about this is that this element is weighted through the research as the third most important element of generative leadership, falling behind the importance of the elements of expectations as well as communication and feedback. This is in contrast to most traditional leadership development activities, in which the primary focus is placed on the development of leadership attributes through the teaching of individual leadership skills and abilities within the context of hierarchical bureaucracies that dominated the twentieth century (Seers, 2004).

Interestingly, in my research and subsequent practice most employees report that the presence of high expectations related to leadership behavior combined with strong communication and feedback processes holds the key to helping them develop their individual leadership attributes. It was not a formal class that helped them develop a leadership skill but the expectations, communication, and feedback about the importance of taking on leadership behavior that helped them develop their leadership practice. An employee may not have all the leadership attributes that they need, at least to start with, but if there are clear expectations regarding leadership behavior supported by regular communication and feedback, employees find that the door is open for them to develop their leadership skills.

The importance of this element supports the need for pairing cultural norms in favor of leadership behavior with complementary trainings that can help to provide the employee with new skills and ideas for their leadership practice. The cultural norms must be in place in order to ensure that any formal and more traditional training in leadership can take hold. I have seen organizations that focus heavily on leadership development training programs that lack the presence of expectations, communication, and feedback surrounding the importance of leadership behavior. In those organizations, leadership training programs sadly end up as a certificate on an individual's wall without any corresponding change in leadership behavior.

Trust

The fourth element central to generative leadership practice is the presence of trust on the part of the employee and the team. Taking on leadership behavior by all accounts can be quite scary and is intricately connected to the fifth core element: risk-taking. If a team member is to engage in leadership behavior, trust must be present in a multidimensional way. For example, the team must trust that the individual is able to take on the identified leadership action and the individual must trust that they can pull it off.

Patrick Lencioni (2013) provides a thoughtful way to consider what he describes as the three elements of trust. The first level of trust is trust in the individual's skills to undertake the activity at hand. Does the individual possess the capabilities required to pull off the project? The second level of trust is that of intent. Can the team trust the stated intent? For example, does the leadership behavior that the individual is engaging in truly support the mission of the organization or are there other reasons at play? And finally, can we trust that the individual will follow through with what they say they will do? I appreciate Lencioni's approach here and think of each level of trust by using the metaphor of a three-legged stool. You have to have all three legs present in order to be able to have trust. Imagine trying to sit on a stool that only has one or two legs.

Good luck—without three legs you have no stool, and without the three levels there is no trust.

From a generative leadership standpoint it's important to ensure that strategies are pursued to confirm the presence of trust at all levels within the organization. Given Lencioni's construct for trust, these strategies should include opportunities for skill development, through practice as well as formal and informal training, consistent and persistent work on ensuring that critical values are shared across the organization, and pursuit of norms that underscore the importance of follow-through.

As you can see, the first three elements within the generative leadership model are also at play in the creation and sustainment of trust. Organizational expectations have to support leadership behavior; there needs to be ongoing communication and feedback; and people need to have the capacity to develop their individual leadership skill level.

The importance of trust goes beyond Lencioni's thoughtful exploration and is seen throughout the literature. Lee, Gillespie, Mann, and Wearing (2010), for example, identify a strong relationship between trust and a team member's performance. The importance of trust is also raised by Burk, Sims, Lazzara, and Salas (2007), who identify it as key to leadership effectiveness. Others have sought to create a comprehensive model to understand the role that trust plays in the realization of effective leadership. McEvily, Perrone, and Zaheer (2003), for example, suggest that trust should be used as an overarching organizing principle within an organizational context. Allert and Chatterjee (1997) underscore the importance of maintaining relationships as a key component of successful leadership.

I have seen the importance that trust plays in my own leadership practice. Time and again I have seen situations where trust is broken between the team members and the positional leader, and when this happens it is a formula for disaster. Trust is fundamental within the team and throughout the entire organization, and if you want to reap the benefits of generative leadership, it will be important to pursue strategies to ensure that trust is present.

Risk-Taking

Risk-taking is number 5 on the list of critical elements to ensure the presence of generative leadership. Now the connection between this element, that of risk-taking, and the fourth element of trust should not be overlooked. Risk-taking and trust in the co-creation of leadership have a hand-in-glove relationship. I know from my research as well as my practice that employees feel as well as believe that engaging in leadership behavior can be risky. They find themselves worried about the implications if something goes awry. They are concerned about the ramifications related to mistakes and how their behavior will be seen by the positional leader as well as their team members. If the risk is seen as too high, then the employee is more likely to choose inaction and the net effect is a lack of leadership behavior.

Understanding the implications of this element underscores the importance of ensuring that there is a strong level of trust in the positional leader, the team, and the organization. When trust is present team members are more willing to engage in what is seen as the risky element of venturing into leadership behavior. When trust is felt at all levels—at the individual, team, and organizational levels—team members will have the greatest willingness to engage in leadership behavior.

Even when trust is high many team members will still feel that engaging in leadership behavior has a level of risk attached to it. For this reason, it is important to normalize these feelings, to let team members know that this is a feeling they may have, and to encourage their foray into leadership behavior, despite it. Again, we see the interconnectedness between the aforementioned elements. Expectations, communication and feedback, leadership attributes, and trust make it possible for team members to risk leadership behavior. Remember that from our practice perspectives it is important that we know when to be antigravitational. Risk-taking within this context is one of those times.

The notion that risk-taking is important in regard to leadership practice goes beyond my own research and professional practice. Frost, Fiedler, and Anderson (1983), for example, identified that ineffective leaders were more likely to be risk-adverse. Weingold and Schlenker (1991) offer another perspective on risk-taking behavior in which high-risk-takers were seen to take on greater risk when risk-taking was seen as a more admired behavior within the group. This connects to the importance of the norms that are established within the organization's culture. If engaging in leadership practice is a risk that the team admires, then this is a risk that is more likely to be undertaken.

Opportunity

The sixth core theme within generative leadership is the presence of opportunity. Leadership as explored in Chapter 1 is a practice that is developed over time. There is a critical need to ensure not only that you have the tools needed to exercise effective leadership but also that you have the opportunity to use the tools regularly to refine and develop your leadership mastery. Imagine trying to learn carpentry skills without swinging a hammer or measuring and cutting wood with a saw. Without a carpentry project, the tools sit in the toolbox and the carpenter's skills remain stagnant or—worse— begin to decline.

For this reason, organizations that intentionally create multiple opportunities for leadership practice are organizations that have a team of employees developing their leadership capability. It is not too difficult to consider strategies to ensure that opportunities are present. Chairing a cross-organization committee serves as one example. Serving as a safety coordinator is another. In my nonprofit we have identified committees, for example, to work on the strategic plan. Chair responsibilities rotate and so everyone, over time, can take on leadership behavior. Similarly, special events within the organization become an opportunity for employees to engage in leadership practice. Becoming a trainer or providing a workshop on a topic that an employee just learned about also serves as a simple example of a way to take something that occurs regularly within an organization and leverage it to become something that helps build leadership practice. The list goes on and on. The key, however, is to be sure that the organization is ensuring that opportunities to exercise, practice, and develop leadership skills and behavior are present throughout the organization. Avoid being passive in this area and instead actively work to ensure that there are multiple opportunities at all levels of the organization.

The importance of ensuring opportunities are present in the creation of leadership practice is something that I have seen as critical through my decades of experience. Organizations that have multiple opportunities for employees to practice leadership behavior are way ahead in the desire to build generative leadership. The literature supports the importance of this as well. For example, the perspective held by Robert Thomas, where leadership is seen to develop best through practical experience, underscores the importance of the generative leadership's sixth core element of ensuring that the opportunity to engage in leadership behavior is present (Thomas, 2008).

Each of the core elements within the generative leadership model build upon each other. Clear expectations regarding the importance of taking on leadership behavior must be present. To ensure that this is true one has to be regularly engaged in communication and feedback about its importance. To leverage the power of generative leadership there must be opportunities for employees to refine their skills through training that exists within a cultural context that supports leadership action. Trust must be present in order to support the willingness to take the risk that comes along with exercising leadership behavior and, finally, the organization must intentionally develop multiple opportunities to practice leadership at all levels of the organization.

Related Subthemes

As noted at the start of this chapter there are also seven subthemes that are part and parcel of the generative leadership model. As with the core elements the subthemes are interrelated. I provide a brief exploration of each subtheme in the following sections to illustrate how they are interrelated with each other as well as the core elements. The subthemes are also listed in order of significance as identified through the research, although you could argue that each has its own merit and some perhaps might rise to a higher level of importance.

For example, you will see that organizational philosophy and practice is listed as the fourth in line of importance. I think it would be fair to argue that this could be the most important among the six elements and the seven subthemes. From my perspective, though, the key here is to develop an appreciation of the role that each plays in the desire to create leadership practice across and within the organization. Clearly, if you are working with an organization that does not philosophically believe that leadership behavior should exist beyond the bounds of the positional leaders, then you will have trouble building a generative leadership practice.

Having a Voice

This subtheme came through loud and clear with the research participants. And while having a voice might seem to be like the second core element—communication and feedback—it is differentiated by a subtle yet significant difference. Having a voice refers to the feeling that an employee or team member has when they report that they are heard, that their opinion matters to the team and the organization, and that they are contributing something to the discourse. I do not mean that they get their way at every turn, but it does mean that there is a sense that their input matters.

In order to have a voice within the organization there has to be a structure that supports communication processes and an ability on the part of other actors to listen. Thoughtful structure creates the opportunity for hearing and deep listening. The ability to truly hear what another person is saying plays an important role in ensuring that team members have a voice. This subtheme connects to the important core elements of expectations and communication and feedback and helps to inform the nature of how the first two core elements should be utilized. If you simply hold expectations firm, communicate, and provide feedback without ensuring that employees have a voice, then you will run into serious challenges and within this context miss out on the opportunity to engender leadership behavior. When employees and team members feel they do not have a voice, they naturally withdraw from engagement. Engagement, as we will explore in Chapter 6, is critical to the nonprofit organization's potential for success.

Interestingly there are a number of authors as well as researchers who have explored the importance of employees having a voice and feeling heard. Google, for example, studied hundreds of teams to extract the secret sauce for the most successful team (Rozovsky, 2015). They identified a number of important elements for success, and key among them was the feeling that team members had a sense of psychological safety and that their input mattered, and that they were free to share and to take risks within the group—said another way, that they had a voice. Lencioni (2013) also underscores the importance of this when he writes about highly effective teams. It is essential for the team to be able to openly discuss conflicts over important ideas and then to come to an agreement that is acceptable for all. Being heard, in my experience, plays an important role in helping the team transition from having unbridled conflict about key ideas to agreeing to a plan of action going forward.

Commitment

Commitment also plays an important role as you work toward building your team's or organization's generative leadership practice. Employees have differing levels of commitment based on a variety of factors. As discussed in Chapter 6, affectively committed employees, for example, are employees who are better prepared to respond affirmatively to the expectations regarding leadership practice. Employees who lack commitment to the team or the organization are more likely to shy away from taking the requisite risk that leadership behavior entails. It is important to pursue strategies to build the right type of employee commitment within and across the organization.

Perceived Need to Act

This subtheme is closely related to the core elements of opportunities to act and expectations, as well as the subtheme that follows: organizational philosophy and practice. The success of the organization's opportunities for leadership behavior is closely tied to the employee's perception that they should participate. Similarly, if employees understand the expectations related to leadership behavior, then they will be more likely to feel that they should engage. As we discussed in Chapter 4, there are several strategies that can and should be used to shape positive norms that support the desired behavior on the part of the team. The one effect of implementing a positive culture through positive norms is that the employee will feel the need to act.

Organizational Philosophy and Practice

The alignment between the expectation that employees should engage in leadership behavior and the overall organizational philosophy and practice is critical. If you are operating within an organization that discourages active leadership behavior—leadership behavior that exists outside the confines of a formal job description—then it will be extremely hard to engender generative leadership practice. If this is the situation, I would recommend pursuing culture change as explored and described in Chapter 3. Ideally the organization's philosophy and practice does support the notion that leadership practice on the part of all team members is a benefit for the organization as it pursues its mission. When that is the case then the effort to realize generative leadership will be more easily advanced.

Role Modeling

In the research it was interesting to see the impact of role modeling on the ability as well as willingness of team members to take on leadership behavior. It makes sense that role modeling would play an important role in the co-creation of leadership, as we all learn from each other's behavior. The presence of this subtheme reminds us of the importance of being mindful about how we present ourselves. Each day in our work we are displaying through action and deed what we honestly believe. As noted in our practice perspectives, it is essential to go beyond "talking the talk" to include "walking the walk." Do as I say and as I do.

Shared Beliefs and Values

As we consider the sixth subtheme, that of shared beliefs and values, we harken back to Chapter 4 and the important aspects of building positive culture. Understanding the important connection between the organization's mission, vision, values, beliefs, and behavior is essential for the success of the organization. Building shared values and beliefs about how the team and the agency's employees should engage with leadership practice is also extremely important. Building the capacity for team members to reward and support effective leadership practice as well as expect the same is critical to the success of the generative leadership model construct.

Structure

Structure represents the last of the seven subthemes in the generative leadership model. And just as you might argue that one subtheme is more important than another, the fact that structure arrives last on the weighted subthemes is more a function of the research participants' view and not meant to limit its importance. As we will discuss in Chapter 7, structure plays an important role in any strategy that you are pursuing within the organization. This is true as well as you work to build generative leadership practice. For example, it is important to consider how you will structure the organization's opportunities to practice leadership. Equally important is to understand how communication and feedback are structured within the organization. For example, is the communication structure one that ensures that the right messages are being received and are the messages getting to the intended audience? Structure plays an important role and, like the other elements and subthemes, it too is interconnected with the team's and organization's ability to engender leadership development in action.

The following table identifies the six core elements and seven subthemes and provides an opportunity for you to consider actions that you and your team might pursue to leverage the power of a generative leadership strategy within your team and organization.

For example, you might want to explore the strategies you use in order to help your team members understand that they should engage in leadership behavior, even if they're not in a formal leadership role. Expectations of this nature can be built into agency employee material, trainings, and other efforts that will help to build upon leadership expectations. Within the major theme of opportunity, you may want to consider specific strategies to build on your team members' capacity to try out leadership behavior. Similarly, you may want to look at formal leadership training programs in order to build leadership attributes while acknowledging that this is just one of the six core themes known to help develop leadership in action.

Core Elements	Strategy to Build This Element and Enhance the Subtheme	Comments
Expectations		
Communication and Feedback		
Leadership Attributes		
Trust		
Risk-Taking		
Opportunity		
Related Subtheme	**Comment**	
Having a Voice		
Commitment		
Perceived Need to Act		
Organizational Philosophy and Practice		
Role Modeling		
Shared Beliefs and Values		
Structure		

As we have discussed, the relationship between the various themes in the generation of leadership is dynamic; there are few if any straight lines between the various themes, yet each plays a role in the development of leadership practice and the nature of generative leadership within the organization. The lack of direct causality does not diminish the utility of the generative leadership model; rather, it provides the necessary flexibility to incorporate the contextual nature of leadership development and the lens of leadership co-creation within a given organization. Leadership given this multidimensional and multilayered approach is more emergent and holistic in nature in recognition of the complexity that is present in today's organizations (Marion & Uhl-Bein, 2001).

As noted earlier I have developed an assessment tool to help identify the presence of the core and subthemes within the organization. The assessment tool includes 39 questions using a Likert scale to assess for the presence of each core and subtheme as reported by members of the organization. The design of the tool makes it possible to assess each core and subtheme at the individual, team, and organizational level. This provides a window into understanding the nature of generative leadership within the organization in a dynamic and multidimensional manner.

I have used this tool in my work with nonprofit organizations in order to help the agency understand the nature of leadership present and to chart a path toward a more generative leadership stance within and across the organization. Remember, experience shows that there is a positive correlation between the level of positive leadership practice within the organization and the agency's overall success in pursuing its essential mission.

The assessment tool becomes a starting point for more fully understanding the level of generative leadership that is present within the organization. In addition, it provides the organization with the capacity to tailor leadership development activities. Generative leadership assessments, for example, that score low on the core theme of trust provide leadership as well as team members with a tangible point of focus as they pursue enhanced leadership practice. A logical leadership development strategy in this context would focus on trust-building activities and efforts, knowing that without a sufficient level of trust team members will shy away from leadership behavior.

Figure 5.1 is drawn from a recent consultation with a large non-profit organization. The graph shows the scores from the generative leadership assessment related to the six core elements within the team category. In this instance the positional leader's scores are seen in contrast to the mean score from her leadership team. Of note is the fact that the positional leader consistently rated the team higher in each of the core elements. As I worked with this leader, I recall the "aha" moment when she realized the extent of the discrepancy between what she viewed and what the team viewed. As we talked through the possible reasons for the differences, she began to share how circumstances had impacted the time she spent in providing communication and feedback to the team. This in turn had an impact on trust as well as on the team's willingness to engage in risk-taking, which in turn had further impact on communication and feedback.

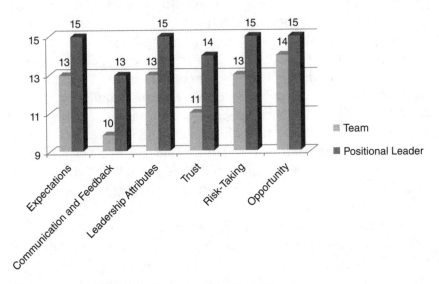

Figure 5.1   Leadership Team and Positional Leader

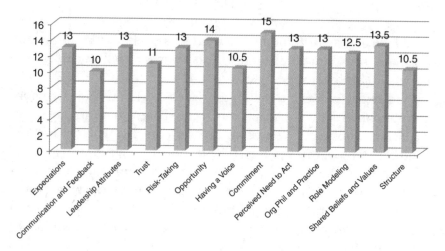

Figure 5.2   Leadership Team: Core Elements and Subthemes

From this point, we were able to move the discussion to helping her to build strategies to enhance communication and feedback.

Figure 5.2 is another example of how the tool was used with a senior leadership team within a nonprofit organization. Seen here the total mean scores across all categories of core elements and sub-themes were calculated and served as a jumping-off point for the team to consider its practice in the co-creation of leadership. As seen in the figure the team scored extremely high in their overall commitment and scored the lowest in the area of communication and feedback, with the next lowest scores appearing in the subthemes of having a voice and structure. With this team I engaged in a participatory action approach that netted a commitment to explore ways to improve their communication practices, their ability to give each other feedback, and to work to ensure that each member of the team felt they had a voice.

The assessment tool makes it possible to pursue reflective practice on the part of nonprofit leaders and team members as they work to consider how they can better engage in practices that support the co-creation of leadership throughout the organization. In addition, as noted, it makes sense to pursue a participatory action approach to optimize the presence of the core elements and subthemes that support the co-creation of leadership behavior. Whether the approach is drawn from Kurt Lewin's classic model of unfreezing, changing, and refreezing (1951); Chris Argyris's model of action science (Argyris, Putnam, & McLain Smith, 1985); or Torbert's model of Action Inquiry (Torbert & Cook-Greuter, 2004); the reiterative process of planning, acting, observing, evaluating, and refining can serve as an effective support for creation of generative leadership capacity within the organization.

Approaching your team and your organization's leadership development efforts through the use of the generative leadership model will assist you in your quest to build effective leadership within your agency. The dynamic and multileveled elements of the model make it possible to impact leadership development and the co-creation of leadership within multiple contexts. The approach also provides room for considering the needs of the individual leader, team members, and the organization's culture, as well as structural considerations, practices, and policies.

6

Performance Management and Employee Engagement

IN THIS CHAPTER we continue the journey to help build a framework for successful nonprofit management and leadership by exploring the impact of effective employee engagement and employee management and, through this, organizational innovation. The hope is that you will use this chapter to support your efforts to be effective as a leader and manager by realizing the power of employee engagement to leverage the important contribution employees make to the success of the organization. This chapter builds on what we have explored by adding important engagement strategies in order to develop the employees that comprise the heart and soul of your nonprofit organization.

There are three interrelated elements that comprise effective employee management that are explored in depth. Each element is important to consider fully as you strive to work successfully with employees. None of the elements can stand on its own, and understanding their interconnectedness is critical to advancing the employees' capacity to connect positively with the organization and to support the pursuit of the organization's mission, as well as the development of innovative capacity throughout the agency.

The three elements are employee engagement, performance management, and supervision. Each area has its own lens for advancing the employees' capacity to contribute to the organization's mission and the agency's ability to achieve success with the people that the organization serves. As noted, each element has its own focus though they are interconnected and, in many ways, dependent upon one another. For example, you must be effective in providing employee supervision to truly accomplish performance management. And as you will see, effective performance management leads to heightened employee engagement, which in turn heightens the organization's capacity to realize its mission.

What follows is a brief exploration of the three elements that comprise effective employee management.

Employee Engagement

Employee engagement is largely viewed as a critical aspect of ensuring that employees are motivated and share in the organization's values, beliefs, goals, and objectives. Mone and London (2009), for example, define engaged employees as displaying behavior that reflects an active involvement, shared commitment, and a passion for the work. In addition, these employees report a sense of empowerment from the work that they do.

Wolf and Zwick (2008) highlight the importance of employee engagement when they write that active employees who share the organization's goals and objectives are more productive. Commitment to the organization is also shaped by the level of employee engagement (Phipps, Prieto, & Ndinguri, 2013). There is a positive relationship between the level of engagement, the employee's level of commitment, and productivity.

I am confident that when you consider your own experience as a leader or as an employee within your respective organization, you will agree on how important it is to have actively engaged employees. Every day we rely on our team members to work to advance the mission of the organization. They are called upon to engage in complex activities addressing complicated situations with challenging participants. Their ability to effectively engage in their job duties and fulfill the responsibilities associated with their position is key to ensuring that the organization provides high-quality services for the people served by the organization.

As a part of this there has been an ongoing focus on the importance of employee commitment. It is true that we want to pursue employee commitment, though it is essential that we work to differentiate the way in which employees are committed to the organization. Some forms of commitment are extremely beneficial to the organization, while there are other types of employee commitment that actually hurt the organization and its ability to realize its mission.

According to Allen and Meyer's (1996) theory, employees develop their commitment to the organization based on the way they perceive support from the organization. Perceived Organizational Support (POS) defines whether an employee feels *continuously*, *normatively*, or *affectively* committed to the enterprise. When the organization rewards longevity and seniority, for example, then the employees gravitate toward continuous commitment. They perceive in this instance that it is the "time put in" that matters and not what the employee has done with their time. Continuously committed employees are often engaged in a cost/benefit analysis. For example, "I can't leave this job because I've earned so much vacation time or seniority and I'd have to start all over again if I went somewhere else."

When the organization is driven by dynamic individual leaders, then the commitment type will be normative in nature, meaning that their commitment is due to a connection to a specific individual or team in the organization. I know you have seen this: when a team member, for example, leaves and takes with them a group of employees to the next employer. In this instance the team was normatively committed to the individual and not to the organization itself. Some organizations reward the employees' commitment and faithfulness to an individual, which is perceived as more important than the agency itself.

Affective commitment, however, is commitment that develops when the POS emphasizes the importance of the organization's mission, vision, values, and beliefs. Affectively committed employees, according to Allen and Meyer (1996), are employees who have incorporated the organization's core values, beliefs, and mission. These individuals in contrast to normatively or continuously committed employees always act when faced with opportunities for discretionary behavior, in accordance with the agency's priorities. Said another way, affectively committed employees always work in the best interest of the organization and mission, even when they are by themselves and are without direct oversight. The ideal commitment to pursue, therefore, is one where employees are wholly engaged through affective commitment to the organization's mission, vision, goals, and objectives.

A friend and colleague of mine, the late Dr. Gene Moore, often spoke about the fact that you can tell what type of commitment exists with your organization's employees by what they do "in the dark when no one is looking." Continuously committed employees for example are likely to simply take a break when no one is looking. Normatively committed employees will respond if they see their favorite team members or boss nearby, and affectively committed employees will not only keep working but will also try to figure out why the lights have gone out.

I recall a newly hired manager who commented during one of my supervision meetings that she was quite taken aback by the fact that everyone in the office was always working. I was surprised at the comment and asked her to clarify. "Well," she said, "at my last job, as soon as the big guy and the other managers were out of the building, it was playtime." She paused. "Here it seems everyone has their nose to the grindstone." It was clear from the description that her previous workplace was dominated by employees who were largely continuously committed.

The ultimate key to the type of commitment expressed by the team and employees within the organization is found in this simple notion of POS. The way employees perceive the support from the organization drives the manner in which they become committed to the organization. If the organization pays attention and makes a big deal about longevity over performance, then employees will see that it is not what you do that matters; it is how long you have been doing what you do that matters. Similarly, if employees see that the organization places a huge premium on behavior that supports the core values and beliefs of the organization, then you will see employees move toward a more affective commitment.

Given this, it is important to think about strategies that will drive the desired POS in order to assure the commitment found with employees and with the team is the type of commitment that will keep things moving in the right direction. It is important to ensure that things continue to move in the direction of the mission even though the "lights are off and no one is watching." Notice that POS is concerned with what employees perceive—it's not about what the leadership believes or about what the board intends, it's how the employees perceive the support they receive that matters. This is why we expand this discussion by exploring the implications of meaning making in Chapter 7.

Performance Management

Mone, Eisinger, Gruggenheim, Price, and Stine (2011) suggest that performance management is a tool for considering how to effectively engage employees. There are several key elements involved in performance management that mirror best practices within effective human services organizations, and so their model is worth exploring.

Performance management is described as processes and activities that help support the employee to successfully achieve their responsibilities and advance their capabilities within their role, with the team and with the larger organization (Rotchford, 2002). Mone et al. (2011) highlight five key activities related to performance management. First, they underscore the importance of setting performance and development goals. Doing this well requires that the goals be developed with the employee. In addition, it is critical that the supervisor or manager work closely with the employee to help them understand how their responsibilities impact the work of the organization. Helping the employee see how their work, as well as the progress they make toward their goals, connects with the organization is critical to ensuring that the goals become meaningful.

The second activity related to successful performance management centers on providing effective feedback and recognition. The manager must be adept at providing an appropriate amount of feedback in a manner that the employee can access to advance their development. Effective feedback is a crucial element that helps in the development of the individual and the team's ability to function. And as we have discussed, feedback is reciprocal in nature and so successful feedback is done within the context of an effective working relationship. The supervisee must trust that the supervisor is fair as well as well intentioned.

Recognition is as important as feedback because it helps the employee to realize their value to the organization. It also serves to reinforce the employee's bond to the organization, team, and manager by serving as a palpable demonstration of their worth. And, for many, recognition becomes a significant event—which, as we know, helps to cement important norms within the culture. Remember, too, that recognition is a form of POS and so be mindful about what you recognize. Does it, for example, support affective commitment?

Recognition can come in many forms from tangible to nontangible rewards and the type of recognition which is most effective is often dependent on the individual employee. In order to deliver effective feedback and recognition, it is important that the supervisor have a strong understanding of their individual team members' learning style, interests, and skills so that the right amount and type of each can be provided for the greatest impact.

Related to the first two activities is the requirement that the supervisor work with the employee to manage their professional development. In its most concrete form professional development is concerned with ensuring that the employee has adequate training. It also means that the supervisor has taken the time to support and discuss career and professional development activities. Of note is the importance of going beyond simply taking the time to discuss professional development to ensure that there is a pervasive culture of professional development present within the work setting. In this way professional development and career aspirations become part of an ongoing conversation between the supervisor and supervisee that is supported within the organization's culture.

Conducting mid-year and year-end appraisals represents the fourth activity identified by Mone et al. (2011). And while many organizations do not provide two formal appraisals per year, agencies should—in addition to the annual appraisal—ensure that regular supervision times are used to check in with the employee to assess how the work relationship is progressing. The key, in addition to having a formal process, is that the appraisal takes the form of a discussion with the employee so that necessary adjustments to the first three activities outlined earlier can be made. In my nonprofit, for example, we conduct mid-year "stay interviews" that are designed specifically for the employee and the supervisor to take time to assess as well as discuss the employee's experience—what is going well and what can be done better.

Process here is as important as and sometime more important than content. I have seen well-written and thoughtfully documented performance appraisals lose their potency because the manager drops the form in the employee's lap and says, "Read and sign this." This is truly a lost opportunity for the supervisor and the employee. Call me crazy, but I have my employees read their self-evaluation out loud to me and then I read my assessment of their work out loud to them. The auditory rendition of the written evaluation provides a natural window to discuss the finer points, support areas that deserve underscoring, and ultimately ensure full understanding is reached. Do not throw away a perfect opportunity for providing effective recognition and feedback.

The final activity within performance management centers on building an environment of trust and empowerment with the employee. Mone et al. (2011) provide a list of critical elements that I have bulleted below. Each element in and of itself deserves its own written narrative. What is interesting is how each of these elements align nicely with the core values and beliefs that underscore a positive culture and a learning organization.

- Encouraging innovation
- Encouraging improvement in work processes and productivity
- Valuing ideas and opinions
- Ensuring fair and respectful treatment

- Listening to and acting on needs and concerns
- Being trustworthy
- Providing resources and decision-making authority to perform effectively
- Providing control over the quality of work

Supervision

Supervision represents the third element of effective employee management. Supervision provides the delivery system for addressing the key aspects of performance management. It is also the stage where employee engagement is most likely to play out. It is within the supervision process, for example, that the employee receives clear feedback, and it is the supervision process that provides the all-important space to develop the employee's professional development goals.

Carpenter et al. (2012) highlights the very purpose of supervision. First, they posit that supervision done well is a strong predictor of job satisfaction. Employees who receive high-quality supervision are most likely to report feeling satisfied within their work. Secondly, they report that supervision done well advances the employee's commitment to the organization. And, as we have already discussed, supervision becomes an opportunity to advance the type of employee commitment desired by the entity. For most organizations the choice is clear: agencies desire to build teams that are comprised of affectively committed employees. Closely related to this is the role that supervision plays in determining staff retention. Individuals who feel a sense of connection to the larger organization and who are satisfied with their work will remain within the organization, contributing their skills for a longer time. Supervision is an important vehicle for both engagement and work satisfaction.

Finally, the supervisory processes become the primary place in which the employee experiences the organization's support for them as a worker and as an individual. Effective supervision will help to galvanize the employee's sense of positive support from the organization. Supervision done poorly, in contrast, sets the stage for the employee to feel unsupported and uncared for.

It is important to take the discourse beyond what supervision can accomplish to explore the very purpose of the supervisory process itself. To understand effective supervision, it's important to explore the purpose and scope of the supervisory process. Morrison (2005) identifies four key purposes for supervision. First, the author denotes that supervision plays a critical role as a managerial function. It is through supervision that the employee receives essential feedback on performance-related issues. Critical here is the ability of the supervisor to assess the employee's competency and to hold the individual accountable for performance that relates to the employee's identified core responsibilities.

The second purpose that Morrison explores is the developmental or formative functions. This purpose is largely concerned with the employee's professional development and the role that effective supervision plays in identifying the individual's training needs. It is also concerned with the development of an ongoing dialogue between the employee and their supervisor that helps to highlight areas for professional development. As one might imagine, feedback on performance becomes an opportunity to pursue professional development plans. In this example, plan development goes beyond the interests of the employee to include areas that are necessary to ensure the employee can maintain their standing within the organization. This in effect circles back to the first purpose for supervision, performance.

The third purpose for supervision is identified as a personal support function. I cannot overstate the importance of this aspect of supervision. Employees within nonprofit organizations face complex situations that have the potential to draw heavily on their affective energy. In addition, life is happening for all employees, which means that employees will on occasion experience personal issues—the loss of a family member or divorce, for example. Given this, the ability to provide personal support to the employee is critical. Equally as critical is the ability to do this without crossing professional boundaries by becoming the individual's quasi-therapist or negatively impacting the ability of the supervisor to expect the employee to fulfill their job responsibilities.

It is important for supervisors to be supportive and play a restorative role so that the employee can be successful within their work. Part of providing support is knowing when to help the employee to seek assistance for their personal concerns outside of the work setting. It also means being able to work with the employee to identify techniques and strategies to deal with support needs that arise from conducting the work responsibilities. This might mean providing some strategies for dealing with a difficult situation, co-worker, or client. It could also mean circling back to identify professional development and training opportunities to assist the employee in their quest for success.

The fourth purpose for supervision is to ensure the employee's engagement with the organization is healthy and productive. This aspect of supervision often appears as a form of mediation for the individual employee with the company. It might be helping the individual to make sure they take their earned time off. It could also be helping the individual make sure that any glitches with their benefits or pay are worked through. In both cases, as in others related to this supervisory purpose, it is important to recognize the key role that the supervisor plays in assuring that the employee's engagement with the organization remains positive as well as strong.

Summing It All Up

Performance management, employee engagement, and supervision serve, at the risk of overusing this metaphor, as the three-legged stool for ensuring the employee's ability to be successful and, most important, to have the ability to support the mission of the organization. In addition, the literature has shown that innovation and creativity is born of a culture "that values the employees, provides intellectual and practical challenges, and rewards risk-taking" (Creating a culture of innovation, 2013, p. 26). A stool without all of its legs is unable to function. This is true as well in your efforts to build an effective team. Each of the three elements plays an essential role. The ability to provide high-quality successful services in a culture of innovation requires that the organization have a fully engaged, trained, and competent workforce. Leaders, supervisors, and managers serve as linchpins within the organization. Their efforts and capabilities to ensure an engaged workforce are central to the agency's ability to be successful. If you can help to ensure that your team members meet performance expectations, have their training and professional development needs met, and experience a positive engagement with the organization, you will in turn help to ensure the success of the organization. Supervision becomes the vehicle for carrying out much of this effort and the skills and abilities on the part of leaders related to the supervisory process are central to the employee's ability to be successful.

The purpose of underscoring the importance of this is not to scare you! But rather to provide you with a full understanding of how the organization's ability to fulfill its mission relies on your ability as a leader, manager, and supervisor. The road to becoming wholly competent within the areas identified earlier is a long one, yet one that is full of rewards. Building your own success as a leader and manager in the area of employee engagement begins first by understanding the three elements and their importance and then by practicing your supervisory craft within the context of each of the three elements. Through your good work the organization will open the door for employee engagement, which in turn heightens the presence of innovation and affective commitment.

The Appendix offers a tool that I use in my professional practice to help supervisors, managers, and leaders assess how they are performing with regard to the three key aspects of employee engagement and performance management. You will note from the tool itself that a rating is provided in each of the core areas using a Likert scale. You will also see that the tool makes it possible to assess each employee who reports to you individually. There is quite a bit of utility to this tool. For example, I've found that supervisors often rate each employee differently in their attention to the core requirements for supervision, performance management, and employee engagement. This is sometimes driven by the employee or the supervisor's personality, and other times by the nature of the relationship. In any case it is important to consider how to heighten the scores across all key categories in order to ensure effective employee engagement.

If you are not yet in a supervisory capacity, you can still use the assessment tool to rate how your experience is with your current supervisors. Instead of rating yourself, rate your supervisor in each of the categories. This will help you develop an understanding, in a more tangible and documented way, about your own experience in the area of performance management, employee engagement, and supervision.

7

Synergy and Management Systems

UNDERSTANDING YOUR LEADERSHIP practice and building a mission-focused organizational culture that can engender effective leadership practice, where employees and team members are fully engaged, sets you on the road to success as a nonprofit leader and manager. As you work to refine these elements of your leadership capability it is important to consider the various systems that will help you succeed. Over the years I have come to appreciate the importance of developing and maintaining effective systems within the agency that support the work of leadership within the organization.

There are the obvious systems, such as, for example, human resource information systems (HRISs), financial reporting systems and electronic health record systems (EHRs), continuous quality improvement (CQI), and employee training and development, and then there are less obvious systems, such as how various departments within the organization communicate with each other, supervisory practices, and ways in which conflict and challenges are addressed. In each case it is important to think carefully about how the systems either contribute to the agency's mission and vision or, alternatively, may detract from the organization's efforts.

There is also a dynamic relationship that exists between the individual personality that each employee brings to the organization and the systems that exist within the agency. When effective systems are present, individual employee personalities are buoyed by their presence. The employee is better able to pursue the work of the organization and manage their own shortcomings, and elements of their performance capability that are lacking are often mitigated. When an organization lacks effective systems you see the agency exist at the whim of the personalities that are present. When strong systems are absent, your organization will fly or fall based on the personalities that are present. A strong personality with great leadership skills will carry the day. A weak personality with poor leadership skills can bring it all to a halt. I have seen this time and again and I suspect that you have as well. For example, consider the organization that has thrived for years under the leadership of a dynamic personality only to see the agency fall apart upon their departure. When this happens, it is typically because the agency allowed itself to become dependent on a personality rather than ensuring the presence of well-thought-out systems.

In contrast, an organization with well-designed and implemented systems will help both strong personalities with great skills as well as weaker personalities with lesser skills to excel. The departure of a dynamic leader, while something that is certainly a significant event, is not something that will adversely impact the organization. The presence of well-thought-out systems helps to ensure that the organization carries on.

It is critically important to consider the systems that you use within your nonprofit organization and to ensure that there are systems developed that support the important elements of generative leadership as well as the development of positive organizational culture, all of which are aligned with the mission of the agency. In this chapter I provide you with some important ideas about how to implement several systems that I feel are central to ensuring effective practices. The intent is not to provide you with an exhaustive list, but rather to help you with a few fundamental ideas that you can use in the development of your own organizational systems. In addition, it is essential that the systems you develop encompass the core beliefs and values that align with your organization's mission and vision. For that reason, we start the discourse by describing several core principles that will help to ensure the success of your organization's systems.

Core Principles for Effective Systems

There are six core principles that I use to ensure that the systems utilized by the organization are effective. You can explore any system through the lens of each principle and if the system you are using falls short in one or more of these principles, then it makes sense to make changes to the given system. If the system you are exploring addresses each of the core principles, then you can be sure that your efforts are moving in the right direction.

Mission Centered

The first core principle focuses on whether the system you have implemented is *mission centered.* It makes sense to consider whether any system that is used or contemplated for use can support the organization's mission. For example, in my nonprofit our mission is *to inspire and empower people to reach their full potential so that they can live successfully in their own home and community.* Recently I had a team member suggest we purchase food for our many community residences through a commercial food delivery service. The idea was appealing, as the move toward this new system would represent considerable savings over the current practice of each residence shopping weekly at local supermarkets, but while the cost savings were attractive, using a commercial food service would detract from our ability to help our participants learn the important life skills of budgeting, shopping, and preparing their own food. The proposal was shelved. It is critical that each system you pursue is one that passes the mission-centered test! Make sure that any system you use aligns with and supports the overall mission of the organization.

Aligned with the Vision of the Organization

The second principle is related to the first, and it is to ensure that whatever system you pursue is fully *aligned with the vision of the organization.*

To do this you have to first know the vision for your organization and then be mindful of how a given system either helps or hinders your ability to achieve your desired state. As we discussed in Chapter 4, a clearly articulated vision is extremely important for helping to build a strong organizational culture. Be sure that any system you develop does not detract from your hard-earned success in this area.

For example, a colleague of mine, an executive director of a non-profit service organization, recently considered outsourcing some of their back-room business functions. She shared that they had done a careful analysis of the savings and thought that hiring out their human resource functions to an outside group would make a lot of sense. As we talked about the possibility, I was reminded that the vision articulated in their recently developed strategic plan expressed a desire to expand their signature service to youth and families from a local program to one that would ultimately operate statewide and beyond. It seemed to me that outsourcing human resources would be fine for their current state, but I could not reconcile how it would work if their articulated vision became a reality. In the end I was glad that she and her team thought it through with this question in mind and decided not to outsource their human resource functions. Better to stay the course, knowing that the extra expense now will provide major returns in the future by ensuring that there is the ability to manage human resource needs internally as the organization grows.

Support the Key Values and Beliefs

This is true for the third principle as well, ensuring that the systems *support the key values and beliefs* of the organization. For example, if a core value of the organization is to empower the team, be careful to ensure that any system implemented does not detract from this important value. I have seen this occur in large nonprofit organizations when a decision is made to centralize all employee hiring and human resource functions. When managers within the field are removed from the process, they not only feel disempowered but also become frustrated with trying to get their program's human resource needs addressed.

In complex nonprofit organizations, the one-size-fits-all, centralized system might seem appealing but could be detrimental to the organization and disempower key stakeholders. Be careful to ensure that the systems you adopt support the values and beliefs that are central to your organization's culture.

Maintaining Both Efficacy and Efficiency

The fourth principle for assuring system success is the importance of *maintaining both efficacy and efficiency*. This principle centers around maintaining efficacy while managing our desire to pursue efficiency. The key here is to manage the two in a way that efficacy is assured. In our Western culture we often find ourselves placing a premium on efficiency. This comes from a production line perspective and "organization as machine" view that is predominant in the way Western culture structures organizations. If you pursue system design simply to achieve efficiency, you will ultimately hurt your ability to be effective, in which case there is no point in being efficient. I am reminded of a nonprofit organization I worked with that decided to centralize all their employee communication rather than think strategically about who should communicate with employees about what.

The allure of a single, consistent source of messaging and the efficiency gained by having one point of communication was so great that they instituted a single-point-of-contact communication system. And while the efficiency is hard to dispute, what ultimately happened was that the employees began to ignore the deluge of daily communications received from this single source. With a 10 percent open rate on emails, some of which were incredibly important, it was safe to say that this communication system, while efficient, was certainly not effective.

There are times when I must remind myself as well as the team that the most efficient way of doing things is not always the best way. As we discussed in Chapter 4 our desire for predictability and comfort often pushes us to desire a smooth, straight-line approach to get from point A to point B. This tendency can become problematic, particularly if it ignores the importance of assuring efficacy.

Building the "We"

As we build and adopt the various systems it is important to con-sider how those systems support connectivity within and across the organization. Building connectivity within the organization is con-cerned with ensuring that the different teams, offices, services, and the various strata within the agency's structure are aligned and part of the organization's overall vision and mission. In my practice I call this fifth principle *building the "we."* Over the years I have come to see the importance of this as an overriding concern within the organization. If you have seen me give a presentation, you will recall that when I say the word "we," I say it a few times and then slowly move from my New England accent to a French accent. Something like this: "We . . . we . . . WE . . . OUI . . . . OUI!" Now apart from my faux French accent the words sound the same and yet they have two different definitions that are, from a managerial and leadership standpoint, inextricably connected.

It is critical to work every day to build a shared mission-focused experience that employees and stakeholders feel a part of. By doing this you work to build a culture of "we" versus a culture of "us and them." If you do this, when you get to "we," I assure you that you will get to *yes*. People leverage their sense of belonging and come together to do the important work of the organization. Connectivity and the idea of building the "we" are important and as a result you will want to be sure that the systems you pursue support the team's ability to feel part of the agency's work.

One recent challenge to our connectivity is seen in the advent of telecommuting that has happened in response to the pandemic. The new systems that have been implemented, such as GoToMeeting, Zoom, or Microsoft Teams, have created challenges for the team's ability to have and maintain that sense of connectivity and to achieve the "we." Because many workers are now remote, it's criti-cally important to consider strategies that you can use to ensure that the systems being used support connectivity. I have seen many organizations, for example, build social networking time into their daily work routines through Zoom or related technology. In these instances, the organizations have recognized that there was significant value to the informal connections that people made within an office setting that must be replicated in this new work environment. It is so important to have systems that help bring people together rather than divide them.

Meaning Making

I have saved the sixth and most important principle for last. And while it is the most important, it can also be the most elusive. As you work to implement the various systems that support the mission and vision of the organization, it is critical to consider the *meaning* that employees and stakeholders within the organization experience as a result of the very systems that are implemented. The principle of *meaning making* provides a window into understanding how values, beliefs, and attitudes are formed and maintained among and between team members—and to achieve your mission and vision, your systems must support the meaning that is desired.

Hurbert Blumer's (1969) classic work on symbolic interactionism (SI) provides a model for understanding how meaning is developed. In his theoretical frame he posits that meaning is derived though the presence of three overlapping factors. First there is the event itself. The *event* is anything that is experienced by an employee or team member. The next factor is the way in which the individual experiences the event from an internal perspective. This is followed by the third factor, *how the event is shared* within a social context. The point of intersection between the three factors—the event, the individual's internal experience of the event, and the social interaction around the event—is where meaning is formed (see Figure 7.1).

So what? Well, any system developed within the conceptual frame of SI is an event. How this event is experienced by the individual and then how it is explored within the social context becomes the core of what the event means. What something means is at the heart of what someone believes and what someone believes becomes the driver for how that someone behaves. For example, I have seen

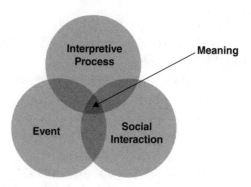

Figure 7.1   Symbolic Interactionism

leaders decide each year to do something nice for their team, such as providing gift cards at the holidays in appreciation for the team's work. In this example the first employee receives the card and feels that the gift card is much less than they feel they deserve based on their hard work and serves only as an example of how their leader just wants to persuade them to work harder. The employee shares these negative perceptions with a fellow teammate, who at first is not sure, but then agrees after hearing the same thought from yet another, more senior team member that this is just further evidence of how this particular leader is disingenuous and manipulative. As a result, the employees agree that they will not be duped into working harder and in fact won't volunteer for this weekend's extra shifts at the group home. The leader on the other hand is oblivious to this and feels satisfied that they have done something nice.

Understanding the connection between the meaning that is created and how people behave is critically important. In the previous example the leader would have been better off to generate a more positive meaning behind their gesture by communicating more directly with the team members about the thinking and intent behind the gift. The leader communicating that they know the gift is not much, but they wanted to take a moment to let the employee know how much their work means to the agency and how thankful they are for their good work would help balance the meaning that is created. Any system, whether it is the informal annual gift from the boss or the formal system that is adopted for the agency's electronic health record, ultimately generates meaning, which drives what people believe and how they behave.

This principle goes beyond considering the impact of a single system to include the importance of considering the systems you use as a collective effort. Taken together the goal is to create a synergy of meaning that is aligned with the organization's mission, vision, values, beliefs, and behaviors. When a synergy of meaning is achieved the agency is vibrant, strong, and can accomplish just about anything that lies before it.

System Principle	Key Thoughts
Mission centered	All systems should support the organization's mission.
Aligned with the vision	Be sure your vision is clearly articulated and that each system supports the agency's vision.
Support the values and beliefs	Systems that are misaligned with the agency's values and beliefs will harm the organization's ability to achieve the desired mission.
Maintaining both efficacy and efficiency	It's essential to manage the upside of each polarity here. Be careful not to pursue efficiency at the cost of efficacy.
Building the "we"	Building mission- and vision-centered belonging helps you to get from *we* to *yes* (*oui!*). Be sure your systems support this outcome.
Meaning making	Use internal as well as social practices to develop meaning. Meaning translates into what we believe, and belief drives behavior. Work to ensure that systems create synergy of meaning to help drive effective behavior.

Specific Systems

Now that we have explored the six principles for ensuring the success of systems within the organization, we turn to an exploration of eight important systems that will help leverage your ability as a leader and manager within your nonprofit organization. As noted at the start of this chapter, the intent here is not to be all-inclusive, but rather to provide you with some important ideas that you can apply to your own leadership practice. Remember, as we discuss in Chapter 1, the goal here is to build your toolbox by helping you acquire some new tools that will support the refinement of your practice. The ideas that follow come from more than four decades of nonprofit leadership practice, and I believe you will find them helpful as you build your leadership and management capability.

System 1: Communication Practices

First things first—first it is critical to consider the nature of communication practices within your organization. Communication is at the heart of everything we do. When things go awry, it can be traced back to a lack of communication or a misunderstanding. When things go well, strong communication practices are at the heart of the success. Communication is ever present and even if we choose not to speak, we are in effect communicating something. There is no such thing as not communicating. Even silence means something to the receiver and, because it is so important, I believe communication practice itself should be thought of from a systems perspective. What follows is an exploration of three elements to ensure that communication practices are effective within the agency. Each element, done well, will help to leverage your management and leadership capability.

The first element of effective communication to explore is the practice of *direct and intentional communication*. This is a simple communication system that if followed will yield true benefit within and across your organization. It has elements of simplexity in that it is easily understood but has to be practiced as a part of your leadership behavior and as a part of your team's practice so that it will be fully adopted as a norm within your organization's culture.

Direct and intentional communication, simply stated, is the practice of addressing communication directly to the source. If one team member, for example, has a concern with another team member, a direct and intentional communication system practice would mean that the individual with the concern will bring the concern directly to the identified team member. Together they discuss and work through the concern. It's only after they have attempted this that another team member might be engaged to work through the concern. The individual bringing the concern is not only direct in their communication to the individual but also their intent is clearly stated and done in a way that ensures there are no other agendas at play.

A simple example of direct and intentional communication is found in this not-too-uncommon scenario between Suzie and Joan, in which Suzie regularly arrives for her midnight-to-8 a.m. shift at the group home 10 minutes late. Joan was very accommodating the first and second times that Suzie arrived late, but now this is clearly becoming a problem. To be direct and intentional Joan simply needs to share her concerns with Suzie and ask her about the lateness, explain how difficult this is for her when she is at the end of her shift, and ask that Suzie come to work on time.

This sounds extremely simple, but for many of us being direct and intentional is akin to the first practice perspective, being antigravitational. We are taught in our society not to make waves and to avoid conflict. We hear from our early years people saying, "Don't be a problem." And so, for many of us something as simple as asking Suzie to show up on time becomes an exceedingly difficult task. Instead, the frustration that Joan feels begins to build up and she finds herself talking to her fellow shiftmate, Jeff, about what a no-good person Suzie is. When communication is not direct and intentional it will not take long before the "team" actually becomes fractured and for all practical purposes becomes two "teams": a second-shift and a third-shift team, for example.

In the direct and intentional communication system in which Jeff hears from Joan about Suzie's transgressions, his job is to listen and then help ensure that Joan closes the communication loop with Suzie. What often happens when communication is not direct and intentional is that Joan will feel a sense of relief after complaining to Jeff and indicate that it is not a big deal and that she does not want to make a problem, so "Don't worry about it." Jeff's job at this point is to ensure that Joan works through the concern with Suzie, even if it means taking her by the hand to help the two of them work it through.

Using a direct and intentional communication system throughout the entire organization helps to ensure that communication remains strong, that the team works through challenges and remains a single team. Each team member can support other team members in working through their approach for closing the communication gap, but ultimately communication concerns have to be worked through with the source. When communication practices are behind people's backs the team begins to fall into various factions, negative norms begin to develop, and the agency's ability to effectively pursue its mission is adversely impacted.

It is helpful not only to decide to adopt a direct and intentional communication system but also to practice it. Team members need time to recognize that direct communication goes against the cultural flow in our society. For this reason, it makes sense to train employees through the use of role playing so that they can develop the capacity to be antigravitational in this effort. Remember the importance of ensuring that the practice is aligned with your organization's core values and beliefs. If respect is a core value that your organization holds, then the practice has to be respectful. Leaders also need to recognize that this practice is one that they will need to sign on to. Leadership has to model as well as accept direct and intentional communication practice. I can tell you firsthand that the benefits of adopting this communication practice as a part of your overall communication system will yield positive benefits. By closing loops, communicating directly, and being very intentional about what is being said, the agency's employees are able to come together as one team, helping to build the capacity for both the "we" and the "oui"!

Open Communication The second element of any effective communication practice is the establishment of an open communication system. A major mistake that I see within organizations is the desire to clamp down and control communication channels. Departments in some organizations are told to keep their communication channels in line, to "stay in their lane" and "stick to their knitting." Employees are discouraged from communicating outside their direct chain of command and can even be sanctioned for this behavior. When this happens, the entire organization can be put at risk. Employees begin to work in factions, build theories (often ill-informed) about what's really happening within the organization, and ultimately can become distracted from the critical mission work of the agency.

I recommend the agency pursue an open communication practice, meaning, in short, that departments, programs, services, and employees are free to talk, share, and reach out to each other as they work to pursue the mission and vision of the organization. In fact, as you will see from the professional development and CQI systems described in this chapter, I recommend institutionalizing open communication practices as a part of every system that is implemented. By embracing open communication practices, you can leverage the knowledge, skills, and commitment of the people who comprise the organization.

In my consulting with executive leaders it is not uncommon for them to share some anxiety about pursuing an open communication practice within their agency. They are concerned about what might happen if people hear something from other parts of the organization that might be seen as problematic. Recall from the strategies explored earlier in this book that we have committed ourselves to developing a mission-focused organizational culture in which the team is affectively committed to the vision, values, and beliefs of the organization. The implementation of direct and intentional communication between each of the various stakeholders can only heighten the organization's ability to realize success. It is important to realize that anything that is seen as problematic is actually an opportunity to further refine the efficacy of the team or larger organization. Problems become an opportunity to refine the pursuit of the organization's mission.

Dynamic Communication Strategies I have heard marketing experts claim that you have to hear something multiple times before it gets your attention. Some argue that a message must be heard as many as 13 times before it begins to sink in (Schmidt & Eisend, 2015). It is clear that any communication you pursue should be done multiple times and in multiple ways. Email is, of course, one option, but it has its limitations. Memos and the releasing of policies also exist as an option, but they too have their limitations. Some team members are visual learners, while others are auditory learners. Each requires a different strategy to ensure that important messages are heard. Given this, it is important to consider how to ensure that your communication practices are dynamic in nature. You want to think about how messaging is delivered to ensure that any communication is done in multiple ways through multiple mediums.

System 2: Meetings

When my eldest daughter was in kindergarten, the teacher went around the room asking each child what their parents did. The first child, I was told, said "My Daddy is a fireman." The second child said "My Mommy is a teacher." When the kindergarten teacher got to my daughter, she said "My Daddy goes to meetings." It's true, in the nonprofit world we spend a lot of time in meetings! Not terribly glamorous but certainly a staple of nonprofit management and leadership and certainly because of their prevalence in our profession, meetings are important to consider, particularly from a systems standpoint.

In any organization there are a variety of meetings that support the day-to-day pursuit of the organization's mission. The key here is to consider how each meeting is connected to the six principles identified at the start of this chapter. Sadly, many meetings become part of a daily or weekly routine that feels completely disconnected from the agency's mission and vision work, where values and beliefs espoused are in conflict with the organizations, where efficiency ignores efficacy, where division versus belonging and connectivity is sown, and the meaning that is developed is counter to the desired end. Mindfully considering the meetings you have and then pursue principle-based action to ensure that your meetings go beyond just checking them off your list.

Most organizations have a simple core structure for their regular and standing meetings. For example, employees receive supervision from their supervisor, supervisors meet in what might be called an administrative team meeting, and, depending on the size of the organization, there is an all-staff meeting of some type, either by the program team or the agency team. Now it sounds simple, but underscoring the simple is often necessary. Supervision meetings should inform the administrative team or management meetings. Administrative team or management meetings should inform the staff meeting. Items explored in supervision may be specific to an individual employee (as seen in Chapter 6) or may be germane to the larger team. Similarly, items discussed in the administrative team may rise to the level of all staff, or may be referred back to be worked through within individual supervision. The process should be dynamic and reciprocal, working between the various meeting forms.

Agencies also typically have ad-hoc meetings as well as meetings for areas of specialization. For example, in my nonprofit we have a safety committee, a conference committee, a clinical team meeting, an education team meeting, and three committees that are the result of the organization's strategic plan. Each committee has one representative from the administrative team meeting who in turn helps to inform the leadership team of the respective committee's work.

Being thoughtful about the way in which the various meeting formats connect to each other as well as the larger organization's mission work is extremely important. Meetings are a huge investment in employee time and resources and it is essential to ensure that meetings are well integrated with each other and that they exist within the context of the six principles as a driver in helping the organization achieve its mission. In addition, do not be afraid to shed a meeting or two. It might be that a meeting has run its course and no longer has a useful shelf life.

As an example of how important it is to leverage the connections between meetings, I recall a newly minted program director under my supervision. I stopped by the program office one afternoon and noticed that he had put up a lined piece of paper on the exterior door of this office. The message at the top of the page asked staff to write down any items they wanted to discuss in staff meeting. When I saw the list, I asked him if he was sure that this was the best approach. I suggested he might want to use his weekly administrative team meeting to explore agenda items as drawn from his managers' supervisions with their employees. His immediate response was "No, I want to encourage everyone to get involved." "Okay," I responded. "Sounds like a plan." I wondered how it would go.

The next week at our regularly scheduled meeting I asked him how it was going. He shared what a tough time he had had at the last staff meeting. "We ended up with about 30 items on the staff meeting agenda. Staff became really frustrated as we only got through about a third of them and even then the meeting ran over . . . Some people had to leave due to other commitments." Furthermore, he commented that they did not even get to the most important items. We talked again about how to ensure that he leverage the connection between the various meetings and this time he agreed to build the agenda from the information provided in supervisions and in the administrative team meeting.

The other advantage of mindfully pursuing the connection between each meeting format is the benefit that comes from building a constituency to help support the effort you are pursuing. Building support, as we discuss in Chapter 8, is essential to ensuring that any change initiative moves forward. As you discuss ideas, issues, and concerns within supervision meetings and within administrative team meetings, participants almost always have something important to say about the effort. When this happens, I make sure to ask the individual with a thoughtful idea to bring this point forward when we meet as a larger group. This helps to ensure that your team members feel they have contributed to the effort; through this they develop "skin in the game," helping to ensure that your efforts to move from point A to point B have a better chance of success.

Meetings should be viewed in their entirety as a system that can support the overall management and leadership efforts within the organization. Done well, they can be a driving and dynamic force within the agency, helping to realize the mission and vision of the organization. Do not throw away the opportunity to have meetings be a successful driver of the organization's success. Done well, you can make my daughter's explanation of what I do for a living a point of pride and a source of success!

As we move into an exploration of the next four systems, it is important to consider the role that systems can play in supporting employee engagement. As Chapter 6 explores, the importance of employee engagement as it relates to achieving your agency's mission and vision cannot be overstated. When employees are fully engaged, they are more likely to go above and beyond the expectations of their role and work hard to ensure that the agency realizes its mission. For this reason, it makes sense to think about ways in which systems found within the organization can leverage employee engagement.

System 3: Continuous Quality Improvement Practices

Early on in my career, during one of my first leadership experiences, I worked for an organization that had a very traditional continuous quality improvement (CQI) practice (at the time, the process was called quality assurance). Headed by a director of quality assurance, the purpose of the office was to ensure that the services and programs within the organization were meeting the quality and service delivery standards set by licensing, industry, and agency standards. I recall the system then and how it impacted my leadership practice. Each service and program within the organization had an annual review in which the director of quality assurance would write a report and provide a numeric as well as a letter grade.

I worked within that system for three years and each year managed to receive a grade what was no less than the equivalent of an A–. Rather good, right? Well, not exactly, because I honestly believe that my program's solid grade was the result of figuring out how to get the best grade, rather than learning the strength of the program and areas for improvement. My colleagues within the organization worked to ensure that the points and resulting letter grade were as high as possible, which I am sure helped at some level with quality, but the system itself really didn't optimize quality improvement practices in the way that it could have.

Quality in this instance was owned by a department, and the goal of program directors, because of the system and how it was set up, was to defend themselves against the outside force of quality assurance and achieve the best grade possible. This was akin to having company over to the house for Sunday dinner. The entire family dresses up, puts on a nice smile, and maintains this posture until the guests roll out of the driveway on their way home, after which all hell would break loose. As program directors we learned to put on a good show, but what was truly happening within the program was a mystery to everyone with the exception of the employees at the program itself.

One can quickly see by applying the system's principles to the described quality improvement process that most if not all the principles were lacking. The system was neither mission nor vision aligned and the values and beliefs supported were not those of the larger organization. In addition, the system might have been efficient by having a single department handle the work, but it certainly was not effective. The only "we" that was developed was the "we" that existed between the program directors as they banded together to get the best quality assurance grade. In fact, the system itself played a role in building an "us and them" between leaders who worked in the field and the administrative team of the agency. And finally, the meaning that was being created was more about system gaming than the importance of ensuring that our services were of the highest quality possible.

The ultimate benefit of this system was that it taught me about what I did *not* want to develop as a CQI practice. Sometimes we learn from seeing what we do not want to do, a sort of reverse role-modeling phenomenon, if you will, and this was the case in this instance. Any CQI system is better served by a system that invites participation and ownership on the part of stakeholders within the organization. Remember, we are working at building the "we" and rather than relegate CQI to a single department, it should be a function that is shared across the organization.

In my organization's practice, for example, we have developed a peer review process to help ensure CQI. A team of peers visits each service, spending a day to explore the workings of the programs. The team has an assigned team leader, and the team works with a tool that was developed by the quality improvement and practice committee, which is comprised of leadership members from throughout the organization. Prior to the site visit the program director, along with their leadership team, develops a program improvement plan for the current year, which includes a retrospective on what has been accomplished during the past year. Surveys are also sent out in advance to employees and to people receiving the services provided by the program to build a 360-degree view of the program's current efforts.

The program director now finds himself or herself with a CQI team of peers that not only understands the day-to-day nuances of providing the service, but also has an appreciation for the innovations and creativity they naturally encounter during the visit. The nature of the discourse changes from passing a grade to passing on and sharing knowledge that helps everyone involved. CQI team members learn new ideas, as do the employees at the program. Using the peer review process makes it possible for everyone to come away with new knowledge and appreciation for the work that is being done. It is also easier to hear from your peers when there are obvious areas for improvement. Not only is it easier to hear, but the advice is easier to accept, as it comes from a team that understands the work being done.

A peer-based CQI system also engages with the other systems. For example, the reports that are generated are available to leaders throughout the organization, which supports the theme of open communication and dynamic communication. The peer review CQI system and the reporting that results connect directly with the interrelated system of meetings. This makes it possible to pursue individual supervisory development goals with program and agencywide priorities that are derived from the CQI process.

Interestingly, we have found that when it comes time each year to sign up for the annual peer review teams in support of the

organization's CQI process, there is a growing number of employees interested in participating. A process that began originally with
only program directors now includes assistant directors, educational
coordinators, and clinical coordinators. With 26 services across my
organization and teams of three or four leaders visiting each program
we now have nearly 70 managers actively engaged in learning from
each other—truly a strategy that helps to build employee engagement
and a sense of connectivity and belonging across the organization.

System 4: Professional Development

Once I worked with an organization whose leader lamented that their
entire professional development team seemed stuck. I was trying to
understand what the issues were. They described the fact that he and
his administrative team had done a great job of assembling a talented
professional development team. The director of professional development had quite the pedigree and was a respected trainer. The three
other members of the department also came with impeccable creden-
tials. They had a long list of seemingly well-thought-out trainings
offered from their main office, and all the pieces seemed to be in place
to assure success in their ongoing effort to engage their employees and
help them develop professionally.

The problem was that employees seemed reluctant to engage in
trainings. Attendance was lacking and even required trainings had
higher-than-anticipated rates of absenteeism. Feedback on the trainings was mediocre at best and employee engagement from a training
perspective was at an all-time low. At the time, the executive director and his director of human resources was contemplating moving
toward a strict compliance approach to training requirements. If you
do not attend, then you are on the road to progressive discipline,
which could ultimately cost you your job.

Now one option for leaders in a situation like this is to take a
get-tough position. There are other options, however, that can help
you avoid the pitfalls that result from simply taking a power position. In this instance the first step in working toward a well-designed
and thoughtfully developed professional development system is to

get input on what employees need and what employees desire for their professional development. A simple well-designed survey can help to understand more fully what the employee desires. Next, pull together a cross-agency, cross-discipline, ad-hoc committee to explore the question of professional staff development and training. The committee's job is to help provide recommendations for how to improve and advance the professional development system within the organization.

Once you have done this, then build your professional development curriculum and the system for delivering it in a way that heightens employee engagement. The challenge that existed for the agency with the lackluster training department was rooted in the fact that the professional development activities were seen as a separate part of the organization, a part of the organization that the employees on the ground felt was out of touch and ultimately had nothing to do with their day-to-day work. A system that engages employees is a system that will realize the benefits of employee engagement, just as we discussed in Chapter 6; engaged employees will go above and beyond. And as we know from the discourse in Chapter 4, building a single, positive organizational culture provides leverage for realizing your organizational goals. A single culture is key, as opposed to the situation with the lamenting executive director's training department, which ultimately had its own distinct and separate organizational culture.

So, how do you engage employees in a professional development process? Well, the use of surveys and ad-hoc committees can serve as the ground floor for engagement. Connect these beginning strategies by providing opportunities to have employees within programs become certified as content experts and trainers for the training curriculum that you develop. An employee who becomes certified to be a trainer in a content area is an employee who is now provided with an opportunity to pursue activities and responsibilities beyond their day-to-day job requirements. The employee now sees himself or herself differently. They understand how they play a role in the larger organization and are now positioned to engage in management *looking up* rather than management *looking down*. As noted in Chapter 6, helping employees understand how they connect to the larger picture of the organization's efforts helps to heighten engagement, as well as the employee's motivation to perform within their role.

Another way to heighten engagement in professional development is to have employees certified to train in content areas join the training team and serve on a committee that helps to review training practices, curricular needs, and employee development needs. The agency's CQI process as well as the various meeting structures within the organization become a source of information for this committee's work, and trainers across the organization play an important role in helping to drive the training and professional development needs of the organization.

Engagement is key and to be engaged one has to take an active part, to have membership and feel that their work has meaning. Meaning that is aligned with the mission and the vision of the organization becomes a driving force within the organization.

As you can see, pursuing professional development in this manner is quite different from the professional development department my lamenting colleague was dealing with. Honestly, it is a bit less efficient, but its efficacy is tenfold. It's important to realize that sometimes, when it's messy, the presence of messiness is not really a problem; it is just the nature of the work that we are doing.

System 5: Retreats and Events

Someone once asked me why I think retreats and events have anything to do with leadership and management systems within nonprofit organizations. I remember my response to them: "If they aren't a part of your management and leadership systems, what do you think they are?" They looked at me and said, "Retreats and events." "Wow," I exclaimed, "I think you're giving away the store."

Let me explain. Within your organization creating retreats and events makes it possible for you to leverage all the elements of culture building that we explored in Chapter 4. For example, we discussed the importance of shaping positive norms that support the mission, vision values, beliefs, and behaviors that are central to your organization's purpose. One of the norm-shaping elements is significant events. A retreat and/or an agency event can, in and of itself, be a significant event, and through this you can leverage the shaping of important norms.

In addition, if you pursue the development and implementation of retreats and events in a mindful way, you can easily develop them so that they sit squarely on the six system principles required to build system synergy. For example, in my nonprofit we established an annual Empowerment Award. The award is given annually to four individuals who have benefited from having participated in the organization's services. These awards are given annually at a celebratory luncheon attended by the honorees, their families, participants from across the array of agency services, employees, board members, and community stakeholders. The event has become a signature event that not only helps to honor the individuals receiving the award but also acts as a potent reminder of the importance of the work done by the organization.

As the Empowerment Award is measured against the six principles for system synergy it is easy to see how this one event perfectly hits on all six cylinders in a smooth and highly effective way. In addition, the event helps to solidify positive organizational culture and creates opportunities for generative leadership and employee engagement. The return realized across the entire organization for this one well-organized and well-thought-through event goes well beyond its annual cost.

Given this, it is important to consider ways in which to design and implement annual events as a part of your organization's systems for enhancing leadership and management practice. The sky's the limit for the type of retreats and events that you can create. For example, beyond the idea of annual participant awards there are employee awards, annual conferences, recognition dinners, anniversary celebrations, leadership retreats, and any number of other possibilities. The key is *not* to "give away the store." Leverage these events so that their impact can be optimized when it comes to effectively managing and leading the team and the organization. Even before the event itself, develop and implement it in a way that broadens participation and engagement across the organization.

System 6: Financial Management Practices

Generally accepted accounting practices (GAAP) requires us to be consistent with industry standards when it comes to our accounting systems in nonprofit organizations. Those of us who have nonprofits that are large enough and receive some federal funding also know what we have to do in order to meet the Federal Single Audit Act, and there are best practices for ensuring that your finance office meets all of these standards. The purpose of this section is not, I repeat *not*, to explore these requirements. The purpose is to explore strategies for leveraging the accounting practices that are used in order to help you build mission-focused engagement on the part of your leadership team.

I once worked for an organization that used what I would call a "closed-book" financial management practice. As a program coordinator with the agency I would have to submit a request for something that I felt we needed and the request, once processed, would be approved or denied. I remember the system as being particularly frustrating. I often felt a sense of not knowing. I did not know what I could ask for and it seemed to create a level of paralysis not only on my part, but on the part of every employee. If we had an idea, we did not know whether it was possible until we ran it up the chain of command. Sometimes I'd feel like Dorothy appearing before the great and powerful Wizard of Oz, fearing a response like "How dare you request something like this . . .Who do you think you are?" We would shake like the Tin Man and run like the Cowardly Lion as we tried to get the hell away! The net effect of this system was one of frustration and cynicism. My fellow managers and I would lament the process during an after-work beer at the local tavern and argue about ways to do it better. The impact was one where I found myself subtly discouraging my employees' creativity. I did not want them to get excited about some possibility, knowing that we might well get shut down. I know that this trickled down to them and resulted in their being less likely to offer creative ideas. Ultimately the impact of this closed-book finance practice system on the agency's mission was quite detrimental.

It is this experience that ultimately helped me consider what an effective financial management practice would look like. Of course, any effective system must meet all the GAAP and regulatory requirements. In addition, it is essential to ensure that the financial management practice system is an open one. An open financial management practice as an effective system to support organizational management and leadership has the following elements.

First, program managers are directly involved in creating their annual budget using a zero-based budgeting development system. The first question explored using a zero-based budgeting system is exactly what the program manager feels they need in order to run the program successfully. This is done before considering the program's funding level. Once a budget is built, strategies to ensure that the income and expenses balance are pursued. In some cases, the program budget is trimmed to meet revenue expectations; in other cases, the program might be approved at a deficit while alternative funding sources are pursued. The important part here is that the program's management has a direct hand in the process and the process itself is transparent. The literature tells us about the importance of transparency as well as genuineness when it comes to effective leadership practice (see, e.g., Bennis, Golman, O'Toole, & Beiderman, 2008 or Tropman & Blackburn, 2018). By being transparent you help to solidify affective commitment on the part of the leadership team and genuineness helps to bolster your leadership skills.

The use of transparency continues within the open-book financial management practice to include monthly income and expense reports for each service, with an agencywide summary that goes to program management. Program managers within specific services not only know where their budget stands, but also have the ability to spend their budget in accordance with the line items. The monthly agencywide budget summary also provides them with a sense of how the larger organization is doing. A program that is doing well is recognized for their support of struggling programs, and struggling programs can see when their plans for revenue enhancement and expense management are starting to pay off.

In addition, each manager meets monthly to discuss their program's budget. Expense and revenue across line items are explored and adaptations are made to ensure that the budget is accurate and as up-to-date as possible. Interestingly this process also provides a window for the finance officers into the working of the program itself. Communication is key and by hearing the day-to-day challenges that program leadership encounters, the finance managers are better able to support mission-based decision making.

Taken together, an open-book financial management practice helps managers and leaders within the organization develop a stake in the overall financial picture of the agency. Leaders who have a stake in the financial picture of the organization are leaders who will help to make the right decisions, decisions that are in keeping with the agency's mission and vision. Knowledge is power and helping to empower your leaders through this is extremely important. Organizations that effectively utilize an open financial management practice are better able to respond to the agency's needs.

The six systems explored within this chapter when aligned with the six principles for success will help the organization to advance its capacity to achieve its mission and vision for the future. As noted, the systems presented are not intended to be all-inclusive, but rather a window into some key systems that will help support you and your organization's work. Other elements explored within this book could also be identified as systems. In Chapter 8, for example, we explore strategies to manage change within the organization, including the process of strategic planning. This, too, could be considered a system, so feel free to utilize the principles identified in this chapter to help assess the alignment of the strategy you pursue.

The presence of strong and thoughtfully developed systems helps each employee within the organization to reach their potential as they strive to be effective contributors to the work at hand. Systems become the point of intersection for the all-important aspects of employee engagement and employee performance. Well-thought-out systems also provide managers and leaders with the tools they need in order to carry out the day-to-day work of the organization, as well as a way to leverage the future state that they desire for the agency.

Given this, there is a saying that I use when effective systems are in place: "Trust the process." A system that works well will ensure that you have a process that you in turn can trust to help achieve the desired outcome. You will find that you can avoid succumbing to the feeling that you have to immediately jump in to intervene. In fact, jumping in to intervene can be deleterious to the system and create a situation in which the team begins to rely solely on the leader to fix the problem. It is essential to allow the given situation to work its way through the process toward its desired end.

A system that works well makes it possible for you as a leader to effectively use your leadership practice perspectives: to be antigravitational, use the system itself to develop your awareness, and take the long view, as well as address the inner pressures that you will no doubt experience as you move through your leadership responsibilities. Remember that a well-designed system is already set up to do that something and with the system, the team has already "jumped in" to solve the problem. A leadership team that I was a part of felt so strongly about remembering this point that we had T-shirts printed that simply said, in bold letters, "Trust the Process! Do Not Forget to Trust the Process!"

8

Effective Change Management

As WE TURN to explore the question of managing change within nonprofit organizations, I have to confess that we're embarking on a topic that can stand easily on its own as a separate book. Despite this, the topic is so important from my perspective that I would be remiss if I didn't dedicate a chapter to this topic. Change within nonprofit organizations is something that is ever present, and nonprofit leaders and managers must have some tools in their toolbox in order to assure their success as they work to serve the agency's mission.

What is so interesting to me is the way in which change, ever present in our organizational work, becomes something that is so resisted in our day-to-day efforts. I have a friend from the north country of New Hampshire who always says, in his quintessential Coos County accent, "Paul, I don' mind change if it doesn't mattah." I cannot help but laugh when he says this. This statement is funny because of the truth found within it. As human beings we are generally interested to hear new ideas and will even nod our heads in agreement until we start to realize that the new idea will mean that something we have always done one way will now have to be done another way. "Wait a minute . . . you mean I'll have to do what?" Remember, as human beings we are hard-wired for predictability and stasis as a way to manage the perils and unpredictability in our environment. Routine comes quickly to us, and to change what we do means we must give up what we have traditionally done.

Given this dynamic it is essential that any nonprofit organization develop their culture in a way that helps the agency to anticipate and adapt to changes that are ever occurring. Changes within nonprofit organizations run the gamut from funding to regulations, personnel, board culture, service delivery models, and beyond. The list is almost infinite, and the necessity of successfully managing change is universal.

Types of Change

One conceptual frame that I have found helpful when thinking about change within the organization is shown in Figure 8.1. As you can see from the figure, one axis includes anticipatory and reactive change while the other axis includes incremental and revolutionary change. The points of intersection result in one of four possible types of change: adaptation, fine tuning, re-creation, or transformational change. I like this graphic because it helps me think about the type of change that is presenting itself as well as the strategy that is preferable for dealing with organizational change. For example, my recommendation is to try and have your team and your organization live in the anticipatory and incremental point of intersection, that of fine-tuning, knowing that there will be times that you will need to be transformational in

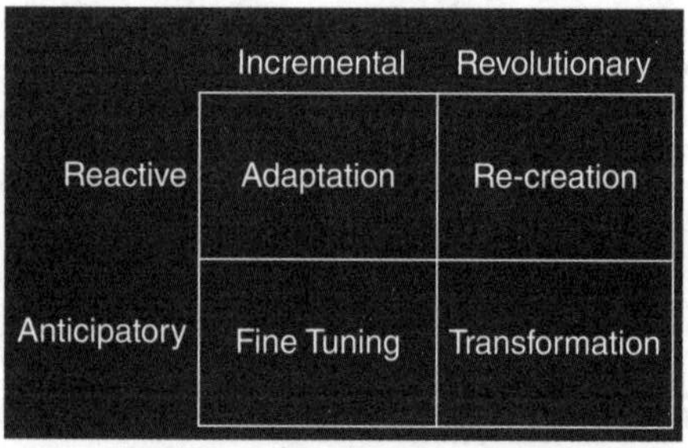

	Incremental	Revolutionary
Reactive	Adaptation	Re-creation
Anticipatory	Fine Tuning	Transformation

Figure 8.1   Change Management

anticipation of revolutionary changes within the operating and organizational environment. Now this is not to say that you can avoid being reactive and incremental as you adapt to changing circumstances. There are reactive changes that occur within the operating environment that cause the agency to be in re-creation mode.

The key, though, is to build your capacity to manage change in each of the quadrants, attempting to be proactive in your approach rather than being largely reactive. There are strategies to pursue change management capacity that we will explore, but it is important to underscore the connectivity that exists between what we have explored thus far and your organization's ability to manage change. For example, if you have developed a team that is actively engaged in generative leadership practice, you will find that you have a strong foundation for managing even the most challenging change that is thrown at you and your team. Similarly, if you have worked to develop a mission-focused organizational culture with strong norms that support the values, beliefs, and behaviors central to the agency's work, then you will be well on your way to successfully managing change.

Given this, it is important to think about change management in a multidimensional way. The ability to effectively move through a change initiative has to be explored at the individual, team, and organizational levels. Each level has its own similarities as well as important nuances that must be taken into consideration as you strive for success in working through the phenomenon of change. For example, some individuals are already cued up and ready to adapt and innovate in the face of change, while others may dread what's coming and wish to avoid it at all costs.

Within the change management field there are seven traits that are widely accepted as attributes that show promise for an employee's capacity to embrace and show readiness for change. Many of these attributes can be cultivated in your employees by using the supervisory and employee engagement strategies we discussed in Chapter 6. For example, you can build on your employees' passion and drive by helping them develop affective commitment or you might heighten their resourcefulness by helping them pursue their professional goals in the area of training and skill development. I have listed the attributes below:

1. Resourcefulness
2. Optimism
3. Adventurous attitude
4. Passion/drive
5. Adaptable
6. Confident
7. Tolerance for ambiguity

It is clear as you consider the attributes that they would help to predict the readiness of the employee to support change. You will also note that these attributes can be informed by the culture of the organization and the team the employee works with as well as the employee himself or herself. If the organization and the team rewards attributes such as resourcefulness and adventurousness, then you will be sure to see this attribute in abundance. If there is a prevailing sense of optimism and a drive present from the organization's culture of mission-, vision-, and values-based behavior, then you're sure to find a team that approaches an anticipated change with the same. Similarly, if the agency has a track record of developing and implementing trainings as well as the support necessary, then individual employees will possess a high degree of confidence in their ability to pursue as well as adapt to change efforts. Strategies of this nature help to build the attributes that we know set the stage for the success of any change effort.

At the team level it is important when pursuing a change initiative to ensure that there is a high degree of communication about the upcoming changes. The discussion with the team must openly consider the positive as well as the negative elements of the change and employees need to understand the reasoning behind the change. Individual team members must, through the process, come to an agreement that the change is worth pursuing.

As a manager and a leader of a team, answering questions about a planned change can be particularly challenging. It is important to sit through any discomfort that you experience and instead allow a full and in-depth exploration of the upcoming change. Allow input, suggestions, and ideas, and remember to be clear as well as honest with the team about the nature of the change and the level of flexibility that exists in its implementation. Some changes are simply foisted upon nonprofit sector organizations while others may be driven more by choice. Help the team understand the parameters.

At the organizational level, Weiner (2009) points out that readiness for change depends on the value that employees place on the change itself. Assessing the value of the recommended change arises from three factors: (1) the perceived demands on the team, (2) the resources available, and (3) the context that is at play within the operating environment. Like our three-legged stool metaphor, the organization's ability to take on a change initiative requires the presence of all three factors. If the task is experienced as too arduous, then the team will not move forward. If sufficient resources are not available, then you'll experience frustration and the effort will stall out, and if the work environment that the employees are in won't support the effort, then you'll also falter in your efforts right out of the gate.

Five Core Elements Impacting Change

Knoster, Villa, and Thousand (2000) provide a conceptual frame that I have found to be extremely helpful when pursuing change within the organization. In their work they posit that there are five interrelated elements that play a role in the ability to successfully realize change initiatives. As you can see in Figure 8.2, the five elements that must be addressed in order to successfully achieve change are vision, skills, incentives, resources, and an action plan.

If any of these elements is either missing or inadequately addressed, there is a resulting consequence. For example, if leadership does not provide a clear and compelling vision for the desired change, the team will find themselves in a state of confusion. In these instances I have heard team members say things like "What are we doing here, anyway?" or "Can someone tell me the point of all of this?" When

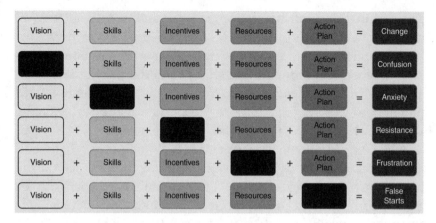

Figure 8.2   Managing Complex Change

Source: Adapted from Knoster, Villa, and Thousand (2000).

you hear statements of this nature it is clear that leadership has done a poor job of clarifying the end goal or desired state.

Examining change through the lens of each element can provide you with a clear understanding of what you and your team need to focus on. You might, for example, have a beautifully articulated vision, a highly skilled team, and incentives in all the right places for all the right reasons as well as the resources necessary, but if everyone seems to be going in multiple directions, you likely need to pay attention to your action plan. Just as when children are first learning T-ball and someone hits the ball into the field, without a clear understanding of the action plan all the players tend to leave their assigned spot to run after the ball.

Make use of the five elements to ensure that your efforts to make a change within the organization are hitting upon each of these important areas. If you do this, your effort is more likely to succeed and you will be able to fine-tune the initiative to ensure success.

Models for Pursuing Organizational Change

There are a number of classic models to help you consider how change occurs within the organization. Each model has its own merit. I like

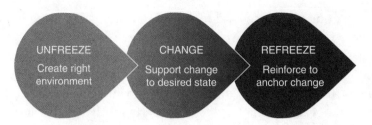

Figure 8.3 Lewin's Change Model

Kurt Lewin's model (1948) because it's quite simple. Lewin believes that organizational behavior becomes frozen in a current practice state. As members of an organization, we hit a particular practice or stride with a given process and it then becomes routinized to the point where it is literally "the way we do things around here." To effect change, Lewin posits that we have to unfreeze the current practice state, change its shape, and then refreeze it in the desired state (see Figure 8.3). Think of the metaphor of an ice cube locked in a particular shape. If you want to change the shape you literally must defrost the ice, and then once you have unfrozen the ice you can reshape it and then once again freeze it. From an organizational standpoint this means you can anticipate some fluidity as you strive to refreeze to the changed practice.

There are a number of strategies that you can use to unfreeze a given practice. One strategy is to create some urgency around the need for change. This strategy is part and parcel of John Kotter's (1996) eight steps of change. Another option is to use a more appreciative approach, where you work as a team to talk about what is working well and what could be done to make things better. Appreciative inquiry (AI) represents one such strategy to encourage the team to change organizational practices (Johnson & Leavitt, 2001). AI can be used to help team members envision a new practice, which in turn helps them unfreeze the old practice. In either instance you are working to create the right environment to ensure that practices can be unfrozen and new practices adopted.

Once you have created the right environment, it is important to support the change efforts. Part of this is ensuring that team members can try out new practices and receive the training they need in order to successfully exercise the changed practice. We know from research that the top four elements of successful strategy execution are, in order of prevalence, the availability of information about the desired change, the ability for managers and team members to have decision rights over the change, to be properly motivated to pursue the change, and to ensure that the structure present is appropriate for the required change (Neilson, Martin, & Powers, 2008).

It makes sense that effecting a change in an organization will require a great deal of communication, hence the importance of dynamic and open communication practices. Decision rights are also critical—I cannot stress this enough. Team members must feel that they can pursue action related to the change, even when that action might constitute a mistake. As we see in the generative leadership construct, employees must have the opportunity to act and must feel they can pursue action despite the risk that the action may involve.

Similarly, be sure that you have developed the right motivators for your team members to pursue change. Some of these motivators might exist as the aforementioned attributes that you've cultivated as a part of your organizational culture. Other motivators might be more tangible in nature. The key is to identify motivators that are meaningful to the team members in order to help them begin to practice and ultimately solidify the desired change. During the recent pandemic, for example, our congregate care units needed to develop COVID staff teams that would be willing to stay in a quarantined house for two weeks when there was an outbreak of the virus. The teams we assembled were highly committed but you can be sure that implementing a strategy of this nature required tangible rewards in terms of hazard pay.

Structure, too, is key. I cannot tell you how many times I've worked with an organization that contemplated a desired change that did not ensure that the proper structure was in place. The notion of structure includes the resources and systems needed to assure the success of the endeavor. Any change initiative without the proper structure is doomed from the start.

Ultimately Lewin's model has us refreezing the system and practice in the new desired state. To do this, leadership needs to continually reinforce the new practice, both by word and deed. Help team members realize the benefit of the new strategy or approach and make sure that they experience its benefits as well. Use your meeting systems to highlight the successes as well as an opportunity to continue your practice of anticipatory fine-tuning. Remember to stay proactive as you move forward.

Resistance to Change

In all fairness you should be prepared to deal with a certain amount of resistance to any change you hope to pursue. It helps if you can build a culture of continual change into your organization's day-to-day operations. Building systems to continuously improve and develop your services and operations helps to keep your team flexible when it comes to responding to change. It is a bit like yoga: if you practice it regularly, you'll find that you can bend and be more flexible than when you first began. Deal with resistance to change by building a flexible and adaptive culture within the organization. When you pursue this strategy, you will see that those who do not like to do things differently will either learn that they have to be more flexible or, alternatively, they will simply get off at the next stop. Better to have these folks choose to move along rather than become fixtures of resistance within the team.

There are other aspects of resistance to change that bear consideration. Strebel (1998), for example, writes about the impact that employee personal compacts have on change efforts. The old "I won't if you won't" adage is one way to think about employee compacts. Employee compacts might also be characterized as a spoken or unspoken agreement between two or more employees to resist or avoid any change initiative. I recall being asked to help an organization build a new treatment practice for the youth they serve and being struck by the attitude that I perceived in the long-term employees. There was literally a nod and a wink among team members. "Oh, sure . . . we'd be happy to do that." Nod wink, nod wink. Of course, the truth was that they had no intention of following new advice and instead had the view that they could wait out the whole initiative until the effort either collapsed upon itself or simply went away.

Employee compacts are generally caused by a number of factors. One factor that promotes this type of resistance on the part of the team is the presence of subcultures within the organization. I have seen this develop naturally as a result of the team that people work with, the particular shift they work on, or the location where they work within the organization. If you hear an employee say "I know what the policy is, but our team does it this way," you can be quite sure that you have a situation in which personal compacts between employees are present—and when they are present, you'll have greater resistance to any change effort you hope to pursue.

The strategies for addressing and reducing the potential for personal compacts between employees starts with the mission, vision, values, beliefs, and behavior support actions we discussed in Chapter 4 combined with the wise use of systems, including the communication systems discussed in Chapter 7. Building on the foundation of the mission and aligning your systems with the organization's values and beliefs will bring the desired behavior to the forefront and in turn will help to reduce the resistance born of personal compacts reached between employees.

James O'Toole (1996) also explores another source of resistance to change that can be found imbedded into the organization's culture, which he identifies as an ideology of comfort. Some organizational cultures develop deep-seated beliefs that predictability overrules productivity, that the comfort that results from doing things the way we have always done things is better by far than creating any waves. "Don't rock the boat," "Stick to your knitting," "Stay in your lane," and "Mind your own business" are all sayings that can be found in an organization that has built an ideology of comfort. I've heard team members and even leaders say, "Oh, I couldn't ask them to do that!" Generally, when this is the prevailing attitude, its genesis can be found in an overriding desire to do what has always been done.

Changing an ideology of comfort requires thoughtful strategies to shake thing up. John Kotter (1996) would recommend that you build a sense of urgency around the need to do things differently. In my own experience, a crisis or a significant change in the operating environment can help provide a meaningful reason for doing things differently. Use these opportunities as a vehicle to do something different, advance your agency's efficacy, and push you further toward realizing your mission. This is in contrast with pursuing a return to business as usual. Leverage changing circumstances to help move from one state to another, desired state.

Edgar Schein (2002) contributes to understanding resistance to change by introducing the conceptual frames of survival anxiety and learning anxiety. He posits that many people resist change because they feel the proposed change is not integral to their position or work, and that they can simply ignore the change because it has little to do with their continued position and work within the team or the organization. Oftentimes there is also a corresponding worry about learning new tasks. The fear that comes from failing at something or making a mistake plays a significant role in heightened learning anxiety. Both of these circumstances help to drive resistance to change.

To address this, Schein suggests that an effective leader will work to heighten survival anxiety while working to lower learning anxiety. Like Kotter, Schein's strategy helps to build urgency on the survival side while providing the team with the ability to access and learn about the anticipated changes. In my own practice I recommend considering that there is a level of survival anxiety that exists around engaging in new tasks that is connected to learning anxiety. For example, how are mistakes experienced by the employee? Is there room for error and are people forgiven for times they make a misstep? Just as we see within the generative leadership construct, if you can help people to risk new behavior in an environment that is supportive and safe, then you will see that employees will believe they can simultaneously survive change and have a lowered learning anxiety.

As we discussed in Chapter 2, it is important for you as a nonprofit leader and manager to develop and leverage your ability to have successful practice perspectives within your work. To effectively address resistance to change, it makes sense to draw upon your practice perspectives in support of the work you are pursuing with your team and your organization. For example, ensuring that you continue to develop your self-awareness will help you manage the twists and turns of a change effort. This is true as well for understanding the inner pressures that you experience while you are in the throes of a change initiative.

Personally, I find it hard to do anything but have a stiff upper lip and expect the same of others. Because I know this about myself, I am aware that when people are expressing their deep-seated feelings about the impact of a change upon them, I have to be antigravitational and resist my desire to shut the door (both figuratively and literally). Instead, I must make sure that I lean into the feelings people have, to open a window and ultimately a door for them to share how things are impacting them. Many managers and leaders find themselves in the same predicament. It is better to listen and explore how change is impacting the team, as this will help to minimize the presence of resistance, and more importantly help inform you about reasonable concerns that should ultimately be addressed.

As you work to reduce resistance to change, it's important to recognize some of the factors that are in play that can help determine the effort's success. When change is significant in nature it can take time to realize the end goal. There is a negative correlation between the amount of time a change effort takes and its potential for success. Said another way, the more time the change effort takes from start to finish, the less likely it is that the effort will be successful. Humans are remarkably elastic in their patterns of behavior, and if change is not realized and solidified in a timely way, the team is more likely to revert to old patterns. For this reason, it makes sense to build short-term wins into the change effort. Help the process by segmenting what you are trying to do to include benchmarks that can be celebrated by the team. This can help heighten the potential for success when a change effort takes more time.

Another factor to consider is just how much effort the change initiative will require on the part of individual team members. The potential for success is directly related to how much extra effort is required beyond the individual's day-to-day job responsibilities. If the plan for change requires a team member to do their job and then engage in added work, you can, in the words of my New York friends, simply "fuhgeddaboudit!" One strategy to ensure that your change effort does not succumb to this factor is to reduce the work that team members have to do in other areas. Being relieved of some work related to their traditional day-to-day activities can have the effect of energizing the new activity. Providing time to explore, practice, and otherwise try out the activities related to the change can help to reduce learning anxiety while advancing the change effort.

Resistance to change is a natural phenomenon. We are all wired to pursue predictability as a way to make sense of our day-to-day activities. And while some of us are more adventurous, we all like to feel competent in our work. Change itself introduces the unknown and raises the question of whether what we have done for so long within the organization has value. This combines with uncertainty about the employees' ability to be successful with the new practices.

As a nonprofit leader it is important to expect a level of discomfort when it comes to helping the team through a change initiative. The ideas in this section provide you with some conceptual as well as practical considerations to ensure the success of the effort. I also recommended that you engage the second leadership practice perspective, that of the *long view*. When you commit yourself to taking the long view you personally prepare yourself for the time that the effort will take for the initiative to be successful. In addition, your team members will sense, see, and hear this commitment from you. This in and of itself can go miles toward reducing resistance. Do not underestimate the power of tenacity as you work through a change initiative.

Strategic Planning

In Chapter 4 we discussed the power of norms, the manner in which norms take hold because we are built for comfort, and that norms are required if we hope to get something done as a group. We also discussed how norms are shaped, as well as how we are hardwired for belonging, and how our desire to belong drives us toward membership in formal and informal groups, which in turn helps to inform our attitudes, values, beliefs, and behaviors. As we think about change management it is important to keep these fundamental concepts in mind, as this knowledge should inform your strategies for success. As a part of this, it is important to consider how a strategic plan can help to support the presence of a mission- and vision-focused culture that is prepared to successfully manage change.

In this final section, I share a formula for pursuing strategic planning that helps solidify employee engagement, mission focus, and buy-in for ensuring successful change management. It draws from strategies we have discussed for leadership practice, the development of a strong organizational culture, as well as the systems explored in Chapter 7. I have used the approach many times over the years within my role as a nonprofit leader and in my work as a consultant to other nonprofit leaders. In each instance, the strategy has been successful in helping the respective organization to chart a path forward as well as set the stage for a culture that is prepared to engage in any of the four types of change.

Step 1: The Gathering

As you prepare to develop your strategic plan it is essential for you to thoughtfully identify who the key stakeholders are, as you hope to build a plan. Each organization can develop their own list of stakeholders but be sure that the list is inclusive enough to be representative of the organization. Some agencies, for example, might be small enough to have the stakeholder list include employees, management, and board members. Other organizations might choose to have board members, executive team members, and service or program leaders, and still others might decide that key stakeholders should include the people whom the organization serves as well. The key is to be sure that you have identified the right people to help in the development of your strategic plan.

Once you have developed the list of key stakeholders, the next step is to invite them to a gathering. This can take many forms but, ideally, you will bring all of the stakeholders together for the purpose of pursuing an envisioning process for the organization. Done well, this can serve as a significant event, as defined in our strategies to shape norms, whereby norms of participation, belonging, and commitment to the ultimate strategic plan can begin to be shaped.

Envisioning in itself is a brainstorming session led by a facilitator. It's helpful to have an outside facilitator but, depending on the strength of your leadership team, one individual can be designated from within the organization to help lead the process. Brainstorming, as I am sure you know, has some set parameters. For example, the purpose of brainstorming is to allow for the sharing of any idea, no matter how strange or seemingly off the mark. When brainstorming, each participant agrees to suspend their natural tendency to be critical of ideas and instead open the floodgate for what possibilities might be pursued.

The facilitator opens the brainstorming session by asking a simple open-ended question, such as "We know we'll be the best nonprofit organization in three years because . . ." The job of the facilitator then is to help the stakeholders to elicit every thought that comes into their head. Remember, since this is brainstorming there is not any right or wrong answer, just answers that are then written in plain view for all participants to see. When I facilitate an envisioning session I make sure that there are plenty of large sticky notepads available so that the ideas can fill the pages and the notes can be spread around the room. This is the first phase of the envisioning session, and it can surprisingly take up to an hour to make sure that every idea and thought is listed.

Once the facilitator is satisfied that the brainstorming has gone from a hurricane of ideas to a tropical low, then the gathering process moves to the next step. This step involves breaking the group into smaller groups. It can help to randomly assign people to ensure that there is a fair distribution of various stakeholders in each group. Try to keep groups to no more than eight participants to ensure that everyone in the group has an opportunity to be heard during this phase of the process. In the small groups the facilitator askes each group to identify the top five priorities that they see from the many ideas listed. The facilitator also asks them to come to an agreement about which priority is the most important, second most important, and so on, right down to the fifth most important priority. Each group should be encouraged to walk around the room together to be sure they see all the ideas listed.

At the point when each group has determined the top five priorities, the facilitator asks them to appoint someone to report on behalf of their group. As each group reports, the top five priorities are listed by the group on the large sticky pads. As each group reports there is always something remarkable that begins to show itself. Interestingly, a pattern of shared priorities begins to become evident across and between the individual groups. I've done this process dozens of times over the years and this phenomenon has occurred each and every time I've either facilitated or participated in an envisioning process. Now the significance of this is important to capitalize on. The process brings together stakeholders from various elements of the organization, many with differing ideas and views, yet the envisioning process helps to develop a shared sense of what is important for the organization to pursue in order to achieve its desired state. A sense of "we" is forming, which you may recall becomes the foundation for ensuring that the organization gets to *oui!*

Step 2: Refining

At the close of the envisioning session all of the raw data from the large sticky notes are gathered along with the group-refined top five items and all the ideas are painstakingly pulled together into a document that will serve as building blocks for what will ultimately become the organization's strategic plan. I generally recommend that each idea generated in the brainstorming session be listed with each of the top priorities identified by the small groups as well. This information becomes very important as the input is sifted through in order to develop the plan.

In this second step, a smaller subset of the organization begins to work each of the groups' five priorities, identifying where overlap exists. This smaller subset might be comprised of an ad-hoc committee established for this purpose. In my own nonprofit we use the administrative team to do this work, with the board of directors weighing in as the product becomes more refined. In many instances it is readily apparent that priorities identified by one of the small groups in the gathering contribute to another group's thoughts while other priorities add an important element that the group tasked with the refining process feels should be included for consideration.

At the end of the refining process the team will have up to three, but no more than five, top priorities to pursue within the organization's strategic plan.

Step 3: The Plan

The third step in the process is the development of the strategic plan itself. The plan should include a description of the process pursued to bring together the various voices that form the organization and then the key priorities within which are goals and objectives related to each priority. As with practice perspective 5 (discussed in Chapter 2), it's best to pursue each of these goals and objectives in a way that is more a compass than a road map. For example, if the goal is to expand your service array in a particular area, resist the temptation to put hard-and-fast dates on each objective. To do so means that starting with the first time you miss a date, the plan risks becoming less and less relevant. The key ultimately is to have a plan that will guide you and support your efforts and not, sadly, become relegated to a dusty shelf in your office.

Be mindful as well about the length of time set for your strategic plan. Not too long ago a five-year plan was acceptable. Today I do not recommend going beyond three years, or even two years, given the changing environment we operate in. Be careful with your time management, though, as a well-crafted plan can take up to six months to develop.

To maintain buy-in across the various stakeholders I recommend that a plan nearing completion be shared as a draft for input from the various stakeholders. Allow folks to look at the draft plan and provide you with affirmation and or suggestions for the plan. I have found that feedback on the plan is a good indicator of how well you included participation. It can also be a sign of how aligned your organization's culture is. If you have folks who have come in from left field, it's a sign either that you missed some important voices in the process or that you have something going on in the organizational culture that will bear exploration going forward. In any case do not be afraid of the feedback, as it can only be of assistance to your efforts.

Step 4: Integrating

So, you have done well. You have garnered creativity and buy-in through the use of an envisioning strategy. Top priorities have been developed and a directional plan is in place to ensure that the organization can successfully move toward its desired state. Now, here is the key: you must be sure that any strategic plan is fully integrated into the various systems we discussed in Chapter 7. Make sure, for example, that you have incorporated the strategic plan into your communication practices. Take care to have the strategic plan as a part of your meeting systems. Continuous quality improvement (CQI) strategies should also explore progress toward the priorities in the plan and your financial management systems should include a review of any resources needed to ensure that the plan comes to life. Each system plays an important role in how the plan will be developed and whether the plan will be successful. Without thoughtfully considering strategies to integrate the strategic plan, I am afraid the plan itself will be doomed to fail.

As a general practice, system integration for any new initiatives helps to ensure the success of the effort. As noted earlier in this chapter, it's best to build new activities and responsibilities into the day-to-day work of team members. This contrasts with continually adding new activities and responsibilities to given team members' job duties. Integrating the efforts helps to ensure their ongoing success and helps to ensure that important efforts do not simply fall off the proverbial truck.

A well-crafted strategic plan helps to ensure that buy-in on the part of key stakeholders is high and that the priorities developed have the benefit of multiple minds that care about the organization's mission and vision. The other benefit of a thoughtfully developed and integrated plan also sets the stage for the organization to be actively engaged in change processes. Creating a culture that supports a continuous capacity for change is an organization that has a leg up when it comes to successfully responding to adaptive change brought on by shifts in the operating environment.

The need to manage change is something that can be counted upon within the organization. Changes in personnel, changes in the operating environment, funding sources, laws, technology, and service delivery techniques represent but a few of the many changes that the nonprofit organization faces each and every day. Developing a thoughtful approach to pursuing the various types of changes provides the organization with the ability to be successful in making necessary adaptations, which in turn support the entity's ability to realize its mission and vision for the future. As a leader it is important for you to help thoughtfully drive the organization toward a desired state so that the implementation of change is normalized within its day-to-day operations.

9

Effectively Managing Conflict

JUST AS CHANGE is inevitable within organizational life, conflict also takes its place as something that is ready to rear up at a moment's notice. Conflict can arise at the individual level, within and between teams, or across the organization. In addition to experiencing internal forms of conflict, leaders and managers of nonprofit organizations can experience conflict that is external to the organization. It can feel like an enemy force with ladders preparing to come over the walls of your castle or, worse yet, preparing to use a battering ram to come straight through the walls, intent on doing harm to one of your services or to the entire organization.

Whether the conflict is internal to your organization or coming from an external force, it is critical that your leadership and management toolbox has the capacity to understand as well as manage conflict. Building tools to address conflict helps you in your role and supports the capacity for the organization to successfully pursue its important mission. Given the inevitable nature of conflict and its potential to hurt the team and the organization, we take time to better understand the nature of conflict as well as strategies to successfully manage potential schisms that this phenomenon can create, which in turn can adversely impact the team and the agency's ability to fulfill its mission.

Conflict, both internal and external, has such potential to adversely impact the organization that significant attention is often devoted to policies, practices, and procedures to ensure that the agency can engage in conflict resolution. Accrediting bodies for nonprofit agencies and health-care organizations are also concerned with the impact that conflict can have on the entity's capacity to fulfill its mission. The Joint Commission, for example, regularly assesses whether an organization has the capacity through policy and practice to minimize the negative impact that conflict can present within organizational life (Woten & Mennella, 2018). The Joint Commission underscores the importance of leadership in managing conflict. There are also specific skills associated with individuals who are able to successfully manage conflict within organizational life. Interestingly, many of these skills align with the practice perspectives that we explored in Chapter 2 and are also directly connected to the development and ongoing support of a strong organizational culture, as we explored in Chapter 3.

As we discuss in Chapter 2, it is important that any leader faced with managing conflict engage in reflective practice to ensure that they have a level of awareness that can help them conceptualize the conflict as well as determine strategies for successfully resolving the conflict. Being aware is closely tied to effectively managing inner pressures, as well as knowing when to leverage opportunity that presents itself serendipitously. Self-awareness combined with a keen understanding of the dynamics present helps the nonprofit leader watch for opportunities that the conflict may present. Trust also plays an important role in a leader's ability to help address conflict. If trust is present, then solutions can be more readily found. It also helps if there is a sense that the leader genuinely cares about the individuals involved.

Consider conflict from an antigravitational perspective. Conflict, when it's managed well, can be a good thing. When conflict appears within the team or between individuals or even from outside the organization, it provides an opportunity to understand a presenting issue in greater depth. Deeper understanding helps to drive better solutions, and better solutions in turn help you to pursue your organization's purpose.

Conflict arises when people care about something and feel that what they care about is juxtaposed to another individual's belief or behavior. There are times when conflict is driven by perception, in which the conflict arises and lives in the belief system of the observer and not actually with the other party. In these instances, the nature of the communication surrounding the situation, or the lack of clear and accurate communication, is at the heart of the conflict. Communication plays a significant role in just about anything we strive to do within the nonprofit organizational world and this is equally true in the realm of conflict management. Paying close attention to ensuring effective communication practice pays huge dividends in the realm of conflict management. As a leader, ensuring that communication is done well, not only by yourself but also by the stakeholders involved, makes it possible to leverage the way in which opposing views can give light to deeper understanding about the presenting situation. There is something to be learned from each perspective, yet if each is not fully understood and worked through, you will have little chance of resolving the presenting conflict.

Communication and Conflict

Baxter and Montgomery (1996) write about the nature of communication itself. They explore the relationship between two types of communication, dialogical and dialectical. Dialogical communication is communication that is centered around a shared topic, where the communication is about shared understandings. Consider Red Sox fans talking about their favorite players. While there may be some disagreements over who the best player is, the fans agree that the Red Sox rule. This would be an example of dialogical communication. Dialectical communication, on the other hand, is communication in which those involved in the discourse have completely different views. In this example they are likely Yankee fans who have just now entered the exchange with the Red Sox fans. The conversation at this point is not just about niceties related to one favorite team, but rather an exchange of completely different perspectives.

So what? Well, from a leadership perspective it is important to ensure that communication within and between your team members actually includes both dialogical and dialectical communication. Full understanding of a given situation is only achieved through discourse that fully examines all aspects of the presenting conflict. Allowing both types of communication enables you to pursue solutions with your eyes wide open.

The antigravitational aspect of conflict comes from the need to move against the desire to tamp down or smooth over conflict when it presents itself. Sometimes there must be a few bumps in the road in order to ensure that a situation is fully understood. Allowing conflict to surface is one way to ensure that all perspectives are heard and appreciated for the view being shared. Managed well, conflict becomes an opportunity to advance how we understand a situation and thereby helps us to be more successful moving forward.

The key, however, is to ensure that conflict is pursued within the organization in a way that helps to optimize its benefit while protecting against the harm that can come of it. Having systems that optimize the capacity for conflict to be resolved successfully helps to build the team and the organization's capacity to be successful. In Chapter 7 we explored the use of direct and intentional communication as a part of communication practices that supports efficacy within the organization. This same strategy can help to manage conflict successfully. Closing communication loops and ensuring that team members communicate directly become important aspects of successfully addressing conflict. Interestingly, direct and intentional communication helps to work through concerns and differences before they can lead to full-blown conflicts. Better to be proactive and address concerns early on through strong communication practices than wait until things begin to boil over (Clardy, 2018).

Core Values, Culture, and Conflict

Adherence and fidelity to the organization's core values also helps to ensure that conflict, when it arises, is handled successfully. When core values of caring, respect, and responsibility, for example, are readily present within the organization's culture, then conflict can be handled successfully. It is important to understand the role that your organization's culture plays in helping to manage conflict successfully. Interestingly, Gelfand et al. (2012) agree that the way conflict is managed within an organization is directly tied to the organizational culture that is present. In their work they identified three basic types of conflict management cultures: collaborative, dominant, and avoidant. Collaborative conflict management cultures work together to identify the challenges and successfully work through the conflicts that invariably present themselves. Dominant conflict management cultures are those that work hard to keep a lid on the conflict through control and containment efforts, while avoidant conflict management cultures do just that—strive to dodge and move away from any conflict that presents itself. Organizational cultures that work to contain conflict often find conflict boiling over, ultimately negatively impacting the organization's ability to pursue its mission. Similarly, avoidant cultures find that conflict eventually catches up with them. The adage "You can run but you cannot hide" becomes true; hence the importance of establishing a collaborative cultural approach to conflict.

When I have seen organizations work together to address conflict in a collaborative way, I always see that the team shares in the mission, the vision, and the core attitudes, values, and beliefs connected with the nonprofit's purpose. To be mission- and vision-focused within the context of the core values and beliefs creates a context that helps give a direction and meaning to conflict management. As we discuss in Chapter 4, the mission becomes the foundation upon which the discourse is laid out. The vision sets the direction, and the values and beliefs become the guardrails for how the discourse can proceed.

I recall being brought in to support the resolution of a significant conflict between two teams within a nonprofit organization. The clinical team and the business team of this nonprofit organization had no use for each other. Conflict had started first with petty issues related to paperwork and had grown over time to include billable hours and differences between personalities. What was interesting about the burgeoning conflict was just how far both groups had drifted from their organizational mission and vision. In addition, the discourse had become, well, just nasty. The first thing we did was agree to some ground rules, rules of engagement if you will, which included communicating directly with each other, being respectful, allowing for differing opinions, and working toward mission- and vision-focused solutions. The divide between the teams had grown wide and moving through the conflict was hard work, but the commitment to these basic ground rules made it possible for the respective teams to successfully resolve the conflict.

In this instance the respective teams had become embroiled in conflict and had chosen to avoid dealing with the conflict by working to establish their respective camps. What helped ultimately was the recognition that conflict was not to be avoided, but rather needed to be addressed.

Lencioni (2013) in his work on effective teams does a nice job of incorporating the need for recognizing the role that conflict plays in organizational life. He does well to help us understand that conflict is not something to be avoided, but rather is part and parcel of the quest to develop a successful team. His ideas align nicely with the development of a collaborative conflict management culture by suggesting that teams, once they have developed trust, need to have the ability to have unbridled conflict about important ideas. Like Baxter (1996), he underscores the importance of creating an environment where team members can share and even disagree with each other about important work-related tasks and strategies. The key, however, is to have a cultural practice that moves from conflict about important ideas to deciding together on the path forward. As a part of this process team members, having felt fully heard and understood, agree to compromise in order to pursue the best path forward.

Leadership and Conflict

Let's be honest, though; while we are wise to pursue conflict as an opportunity to have the team learn and grow as well as develop new and more successful strategies to use in pursuit of the agency's mission, there are times when it represents a clear and present danger to the organization. When the conflict is fully entrenched within the organization and when the individuals involved refuse to work toward resolution, the organization is truly at risk. This is the reason so many accrediting bodies within the nonprofit field focus on the agency's capacity to resolve conflict. Conflict that is unchecked not only impacts the organization's ability to pursue its mission, but also can cause harm to the people being served by the nonprofit organization.

For this reason, it is critical that leadership within the organization have the skills necessary to manage situations from the point of conflict to full resolution. One necessary skill is to know when to step in and provide clear boundaries and limits so that the conflict can be successfully resolved. The clinical and administrative team that was in conflict together had the benefit of a wise leader who set the tone that ultimately resulted in my involvement. They had done what they could to help resolve the challenges existing between the two teams and they knew enough to realize when an intervention was necessary. They ultimately set a limit and moved into a Tell mode with the two teams, letting them know that the current state of affairs was unacceptable and would need to be resolved.

The work that we did was pursued within the context of the limits that the leader set. By telling the respective teams that this would have to be addressed and by arranging for an external consultant, the leader created the context for the conflict resolution. In Chapter 3 we explored Tannenbaum and Schmidt's (1973) classic model for choosing a leadership style. Viewing conflict through this lens is extremely helpful. In the case example, the leader held greater knowledge as to the threat that the ongoing conflict held to the entire organization and, as a result, she moved into a Tell mode. This is not to be confused with aforementioned dominant conflict management culture, in which the leader works to tamp down conflict through power and control. In this instance, the leader took control in order to set a course so that the team could then move forward and out of the conflict-ridden context.

In many ways leadership in this example is pursuing what Drucker termed simultaneous loose-tight controls (Drucker, 2006). Leaders who engage in simultaneous loose-tight controls are leaders who help the team understand what is nonnegotiable as well as where there is room for the team to engage in action. The nonnegotiable or tight elements as laid out by the leader for the team were that the existing conflict had to be resolved and that the respective teams would participate in a process to do just that. The loose elements had to do with the way in which the challenge was worked through.

Another important concept related to conflict management has to do with the boundary function of leadership, particularly when the conflict itself is one that is external to the organization. The boundary function of leadership is concerned with maintaining the boundaries necessary for team members and employees to conduct their work. Consider regulatory bodies, for example. They have authority over your organization, but the way in which they express this authority must ensure that your team remains able to conduct its work. As a leader, pay attention to how this authority is exercised. Do the regulators knock at the front door and wait politely to be brought in, or do they climb in through the windows at all hours of the day and night? Helping to maintain boundaries, which include expectations and practices for access and engagement, are key to ensuring that your team can continue to function during a time of conflict.

Table 9.1 provides a quick view of key conflict management strategies.

One thing is certain: you will experience conflict within your organization. Given this, the strategies that we have explored are critically important to ensure the agency's success. Taken together they provide you with a way to work toward successful outcome and conflict resolution. It is important to consider that even in the most conflictual circumstance, people generally have more in common with each other than they have differences. Thoughtful and well-developed conflict resolution strives to heighten this fact, as you work through the differences that exist. And when you are in the thick of it, and it feels messy, remember, just as I referenced in Chapter 7, when it is messy it often means you are actually doing the work and making progress toward your desired goal.

Table 9.1   Conflict Management Strategies

	Key Elements
Proactive engagement	Stay ahead of conflict by ensuring that challenges and issues are addressed early on.
Communication	Practice direct and intentional communication to ensure loops are closed and feedback is provided directly to those involved. Support dialectical as well as dialogical communication. Work to break down assumptions and provide clear understanding about differing perspectives.
Mission focused	Stick to the mission. Ensure that conflict resolution helps to support mission-focused behavior.
Leadership skills	Build on your practice perspectives. Work to develop trust and genuineness. Know when to tell, sell, consult, and join. Practice loose-tight controls.
Operationalize conflict	Include expectations that conflict will happen and that it will be resolved, resulting in compromise and commitment for a path forward.
Boundary function of leadership	Help define roles and responsibilities. Make sure to set standards for boundaries so that team members can pursue the work.
Build collaborative culture	Develop norms that support problem solving and teamwork toward mission-based solutions during times of conflict (and throughout day-to-day work activities).
Values- and beliefs-focused	Build strong values and beliefs within your organization's operations that can be drawn upon to support conflict resolution. Operationalize values such as respect, caring, and responsibility.

(Continued)

Table 9.1   (Continued)

	Key Elements
Conflict as opportunity	Conflict can serve as an opportunity to learn and grow, to consider alternative ways of doing things. Avoid tamping and smoothing out conflict. Choose instead to lean into conflict and explore the presenting situation as an opportunity for learning and growth.
Vision work	Connect conflict resolution to the organization's vision. Ensure that solutions are aligned with the agency's vision.

10

Leadership Strategies
for Effective Teams

Your success as a nonprofit leader and manager depends on several factors. As we discussed in earlier chapters, you need to develop your leadership practice, build a leadership toolbox, and utilize strategies that will help ensure that your organization's culture is strong. You will also want to help build a generative leadership practice across the organization in which individual employees are afforded the capacity to engage in leadership behavior within their role. Employee engagement also serves to build success, and the systems you use must help weave all these elements together.

Key is the ability to develop and support the presence of a high-quality team within the agency. High-quality teams are teams where individual employees have committed themselves to work together to advance the mission and vision of the organization. A high-quality team is committed first and foremost to the agency's mission and vision, followed closely by a commitment to support each other in realizing the work of the agency. The success of your leadership will rise and fall based on the strength of your team. The stronger your team, the more effective you will be in your role as a nonprofit manager and leader. Given this, it is important to take time to explore strategies to develop and maintain a high-quality team.

To be clear, everyone wants to have an effective team. Who can argue the importance of having a team that will go the distance, help where help is needed, go beyond what is expected, learn, grow, and ultimately act in the best interests of the organization? No one says "Gee, I'd really like to have a team that is dysfunctional, never gets done what it needs to, and causes me to lie awake at night wondering how things will ever work out." While we all want to have a highly functional team, it is odd that for many organizations this remains an elusive goal. In this chapter the intent is to share some strategies to help you and your team achieve what you genuinely want. We will explore the notion of effective teams at a number of levels starting with first things first, and that is to take some time to help you engage in some self-reflection about your own supervisory style.

Self-Reflection: Your Supervisory Style

As we build upon our framework for successful teams, it is only fair that we revisit the practice perspectives that are central to your own leadership skills. For example, it is important to explore just how aware you are of your supervisory style. Successful supervisors have the ability to empower their team members, helping to raise them up and build on their strengths. They can also take a challenge presented by a team member's shortcomings and make it an opportunity for improvement. Successful supervisors understand how to help their team members shine as heroes rather than stepping in and taking the spotlight themselves. As we discussed in Chapter 6, supervisors who are successful utilize multiple strategies to engage and support their team member's performance. Consider the following questions and rate yourself for how you believe you perform for each, with a 5 being superb and a 1 showing the greatest need for growth.

Question	Rating: 5 = Superb, 1 = Greatest Room for Growth
I regularly work to empower my team members.	
I work from my team members' strengths.	
When there are problems, I look for opportunities for team members to improve.	
I always listen to my team members when they share a concern with me.	
I always acknowledge my team members' successes.	
When I'm complimented for my work, I let the complimenter know that my team's efforts are the secret to my success.	
I regularly give feedback to my team members.	
I regularly seek feedback about my supervisory style from my team.	

To be fair, one of the challenges we face is just how tricky awareness can be. I have worked with many individuals who rate themselves extremely high in each of this table's categories only to find that their team would rate them quite a bit lower. In truth, I have even sat with a team where a supervisor was talking about their score from conducting this simple assessment only to pick up on the subtle nonverbals on the part of their fellow teammates. You know what I mean, the eyebrow that gets raised slightly or the eyes that roll up into somebody's head when someone who really does not listen proclaims that they do. Given the tricky nature of truly being aware, it is important to recognize that we are all at risk of being caught unaware. The key is to build in strategies for feedback to help you regularly fine-tune your own awareness. Feedback can come by soliciting it from your team members, from the systems you build, as discussed in Chapter 7, from surveys, and from your own supervisor and/or mentor. The key here is to ensure that you have ways to receive feedback so that you can heighten your awareness and build upon your skills as a supervisor and leader, which in turn helps to grow your team's capacity to be successful.

Building Awareness at the Team and Individual Levels

There is a classic model developed by Joseph Luft and Harry Ingham (1955), known as the Johari window, that is quite useful when it comes to understanding the dynamics of awareness, particularly within the context of the team. Figure 10.1 shows two axes that help determine four conditions that are present within the workings of a team. The first axis is what is known or unknown to oneself, and the second axis is what is known or unknown to others. The premise of the model is that each of the four conditions pictured—Open, Blind, Hidden, and Unknown—are the result of what is either known or unknown to oneself and known or unknown to others. For example, you know that I am the author of this book, and I know it, too! Using the Johari window this fact would fall in the Open quadrant. Now there may be something that you have realized about me from reading this book that

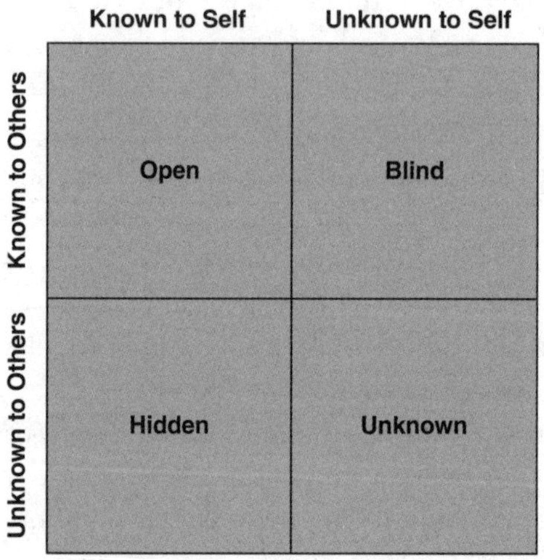

	Known to Self	Unknown to Self
Known to Others	Open	Blind
Unknown to Others	Hidden	Unknown

Figure 10.1   Johari Window

I am unaware of. In that case we are talking about something that falls in the Blind quadrant. Anything in the Hidden quadrant is something that I know about myself that you do not know about me, and the Unknown quadrant is anything that neither of us knows about me.

The key here, when working from a team standpoint, is to strive, using effective feedback practices as described in the sixth practice perspective of awareness, to expand the open area between team members. Team members who have a higher degree of open area between them can better support each other to work more effectively to fulfill their responsibilities and ultimately be more successful. I recall, for example, working with a team in a residential treatment program for youth and we knew that one of the team members was incredibly gifted with helping the young women within the program work through crisis situations. We also knew that one staff person was completely inexperienced in this area. By having this knowledge in the open we were able to use team skills appropriately as well as develop training and development strategies for the less experienced staff person.

Now, if in the same situation these dynamics fell into the hidden or unknown quadrant, the team would have had difficulties as they worked to help when there was a crisis. For example, imagine if the inexperienced staff person was afraid to ask for help with difficult situations. Their fear creates a context where they would hide their inexperience from their team members. In this instance something could easily go very wrong the next time this team member tried to intervene within a crisis situation. Going back to the example of the supervisor who does not listen very well: if his or her need to develop listening skills existed within the Open quadrant, meaning that the supervisor and the team members know that this is a goal, then the entire team will ultimately function better together.

Hidden areas typically are driven by fear on the part of team members that can be influenced by a number of factors. As we discussed in Chapter 2, inner pressures can drive team members to hold back and expand the hidden quadrant. Their own history might make them inclined to avoid the risk of failure or feel ashamed if they lack skill in a particular area. Another factor can be the way in which the team and/or the supervisor deals with shortcomings or areas for growth. If you scored low in the assessment of your supervisory style in your ability to look for opportunities for growth when team members have a problem, then there is a strong likelihood that your team members will prefer to hide their shortcomings from you. Conversely, if failings are seen as an opportunity to develop, then the Hidden quadrant will be smaller and the Open quadrant larger. The goal to increase the Open area should be focused on agency- and work-related activity, as some things should stay hidden and not in the open, such as some personal information.

You might wonder how to reduce the Unknown in order to build on the Open. When I first began to work with the Johari window model, this question always presented a quandary for me. After all, if something is truly unknown, how can you possibly know about it? Over time, however, I have come to appreciate how the items in the Unknown quadrant can be discovered and added to the Open quadrant. The key is to build a culture of discovery within the team. For example, teams that have a practice of trying new responsibilities between and among team members are teams that are better able to discover the Unknown. Being able to try out new tasks and responsibilities becomes a key for self-knowledge as well as team discovery. I am reminded immediately of team members who never knew they could become successful trainers until they were given the opportunity to try it out. Not only did they discover that they had a skill for public speaking, but we also discovered that the employees had a special knack for working a crowd. Today these individuals are a regular part of my nonprofit's training program, and the training program is better for it because we worked together to help discover a skill that had been unknown to all involved.

As a supervisor and team leader, the Johari window model becomes a useful tool for conceptualizing the dynamics within the team as well as an envisioned state that you desire to achieve with your employees. The goal, as we have discussed, is to grow the open area by reducing each of the other quadrants. For example, you can reduce the unknown through exploration and skill development, reduce the hidden by creating an environment where team members feel safe to share their vulnerabilities, and reduce the blind by ensuring that the team dynamic is such that trust is high and team members are willing to provide each other with feedback.

I have also found the tool useful as a conceptual frame for the team to work toward. I have learned from working with teams that are stuck that it's helpful to present the model and then engage in a deep dive into the dynamics that are present within the team. Helping the team talk about strategies to build their ability to be open with each other provides a path forward that supports the development of positive norms that will support the growth of the Open quadrant. Asking the following questions can help facilitate this effort.

Blind Quadrant

1. Are we able to give each other feedback about work-related efforts?
2. Am I open to receiving feedback from my team members?
3. Do I ask for feedback from my team members so that I can be a better team member?
4. When I hear something from a colleague that is uncomfortable, do I get defensive?
5. What are three strategies that we can work on together to help enhance our ability to give feedback?

Unknown Quadrant

1. Am I willing to take on new tasks and/or responsibilities?
2. Does our team provide opportunities for members to take on new tasks or responsibilities?
3. When a team member takes on a new responsibility, are they provided with the training needed?
4. As a team, are we willing to risk taking on new responsibilities?
5. Do we recognize team members for the skills that they are developing that were heretofore unknown to us?

Hidden Quadrant

1. Do I feel safe to share my weaknesses with my supervisor?
2. Do we communicate openly as a team or are there team members who are holding back?

3. Do we regularly talk about each team member's areas for growth?
4. Do we talk about the team's strengths and areas for growth?

Open Quadrant

1. Does the team have a clear understanding of each team member's strengths and weaknesses?
2. Do we regularly discuss strategies to build the Open quadrant?
3. What are three strategies we can use to continue to expand the Open quadrant?

Understand Parallel Process

As you work to build your team it is important to understand the dynamics that are present within the team. The dynamics that exist have their genesis in the makeup of your individual team members, the normative culture that has been developed within the team as well as in the larger organization, and the way your supervisory skills are manifest in the day-to-day engagement with team members. Another factor that influences the dynamics within the team is the conceptual frame of parallel process.

Parallel process, for the purposes of our discussion, is a simple yet powerful phenomenon that influences the dynamics within the team as well as the larger organization. Simply stated, parallel process is the phenomenon where one process at one level within the organization will be seen to permeate other layers within the organization. Consider, for example, the supervisor who regularly berates his team members. What you find within the context of parallel process is that this behavior becomes replicated down the line. The supervisor berates the team member and the team member in turn berates their subordinate or, worse, the individual being served by the organization. It does not matter, for example, if the team professes the importance of valuing everyone's contribution; it is ultimately the process that the team experiences that drives the processes further down the line.

Parallel process can flow up, down, or across the organization just as easily. For example, when I served as the director of a residential treatment school, I began to hear from my supervisees that the children had stopped talking in treatment groups. By the time I had heard this from a third employee, I added it to the staff meeting agenda. When the item came up on the agenda, I explained that I had heard that the children were not making use of treatment groups, that they had essentially fallen silent, and that this was a concern expressed by a number of team members. When I asked for input from the team I was struck by the silence. It was quite remarkable in that the silence was deafening and ultimately an indication that there was a parallel process at play.

Ultimately, we realized that changes in the team membership, including the addition of new employees and the departure of long-term team members, had created a dynamic where even the employees had stopped talking with each other. The children were simply responding to the process that was present within the staff team. Once we began to work on our own capacity to talk and work through the challenges encountered by the staff, the children began to make use of their treatment groups once again.

It is important to pay attention to the phenomenon of parallel process. You can be sure that any process you engage in will permeate the other layers of the organization. Given this, it is critical to be mindful of the processes that you engage in. Do you say what you do and do what you say? If you are striving, for example, to have open and direct communication within and across the organization, do you practice this process yourself? If you do, then you will help to ensure that this process will be mirrored throughout the various levels of the organization. If you do not, then I can guarantee you that your team, as well as the various levels of the organization, will not as well.

Understanding the phenomenon of parallel process will give you a leg up in understanding the dynamics that are present within the team and across the organization. It also provides a useful frame for considering the impact of any process that you plan to implement.

Get the Right People in the Right Place

Having the right people on the team in the right place will help to ensure the success of your efforts. Collins (2001) talks about having the right people on the bus in the right seats in order to get the job done.

Expanding upon the metaphor, it is also important to know when it is time for someone to get off the bus. It can become quite problematic when someone has missed their stop altogether and as a result begins to negatively impact the rest of the team.

In my experience the right people are team members who are "all in." They are affectively committed to the organization (Allen & Meyer, 1996). As a result, they share in the mission and vision of the agency and the way they engage every day is aligned with the core values of the organization. In addition, they are willing to learn and grow and possess a level of courage that helps them to be fully engaged in generative leadership practice. They may also possess specialized skills related to their role and have a dedication to excellence in their work performance. If they do not have all the skills, they are actively working to develop them.

From an interpersonal standpoint, the right people also have the ability to engage positively with their colleagues. They work to solve problems and are good communicators. They see the big picture and have the ability to recognize the important role that each team member plays in fulfilling the organization's mission.

As a supervisor you are golden if you have the right people in the right place. It is true though that this is not always the case. In many instances you may find that a team member possesses some of these important attributes, but not all of them. Do not worry, as there are strategies that you can leverage to help develop your team members. Many of the strategies explored in our chapter on organizational culture (Chapter 4), generative leadership (Chapter 5), and performance management and engagement (Chapter 6) will help to support the skills you desire in your team members. In addition, there are a few other strategies that I explore here.

Allow for Ownership

One of the first strategies that comes to mind is the power of employee ownership. You can help to develop the right people by ensuring that you allow employees to have a sense of ownership for their role and their responsibilities. This is accomplished in several ways. One way to ensure ownership when an employee has taken on a responsibility or duty is to be sure that you, as the supervisor, simply get out of the way. Allow the team member to manage the responsibility. As they develop their skills and capabilities they will also begin to contribute to the work in their own way. Part of getting out of the way is allowing the team member to contribute to the particular responsibility by enhancing the practice, as well as suggesting and adopting changes in the practice.

Sometimes as a supervisor we are so concerned about things going well that we end up jumping in and taking control at the first sign of trouble. If you jump in and take over, you adversely impact employee ownership in three ways. First, your employees will become accustomed to your intervention and as a result they will not truly take on the responsibility. Instead, they will pursue the effort half-heartedly, knowing that things will soon be taken out of their hands. This connects to the second adverse impact. When you jump in and take over, the employee won't actually learn, never mind master, the activities related to the responsibility, and, finally, supervisors who jump in and take over send a message: "I'd rather do it myself and have it done right the first time." This is perhaps one of the more detrimental adverse impacts that can result from not knowing how to get out of the way and allowing your team member to fulfill the responsibility you have asked them to.

Be sure to get out of the way and allow your employee to take on the responsibility. Mistakes will happen and things may not be completely the way that you would like them done. It's better to help your employees to live and learn, knowing that the process itself will help the team member build a sense of ownership and become a stronger team member.

Support in the Right Amount at the Right Time

Now there is a delicate balance between allowing for ownership and this next strategy: to know when to provide support in the right amount at the right time. Knowing when to lean in and help and when to lean back and allow the process to unfold is key. If you are too involved, you'll interfere with the employees' ability to take ownership, yet if you miss the point where you should be involved, you risk causing the team member to feel abandoned and unnecessarily discouraged. In many ways your success with this balancing act is the result of practice over time.

Achieving this balance is often the result of ensuring that you have a clear communication and feedback process established with your team member and that you know the skills and characteristics of the team member involved. Do they, for example, understand their strengths and limitations, and are they willing to reach out if they find themselves in over their heads, or are they lacking in their own self-awareness and reticent to reach out when they are going under? Clearly, the way you provide support and when you provide it will be different based on the characteristics, skills, and abilities that are present with the individual team member.

The Right Tools and Training

It is important to develop clear expectations, goals, and objectives for your team and once you have done this it is equally important to ensure that you've provided your team with the tools and training necessary to assure success. Any initiative that you pursue will falter and ultimately fail if the right tools and proper training are not in place. Many supervisors are adept at setting up expectations, goals, and objectives, but then they drop the ball when it comes to fully resourcing the team for success. Some supervisors lay out the goals and objectives and then go behind closed doors and hope for the best. When this happens, it can be a function of the manager being unsure of the tools and training that are needed for success. Other times it is a function of the parallel process that develops when upper management has let the supervisor know that there are no additional resources available, yet the job must be done. And still other times this behavior is driven by poor communication practices that are already at play within the team's culture.

In any case, when this happens the ability for an underresourced and poorly trained team to fully perform is under significant duress. In this context the team may perform for a period of time, but the lack of resources will ultimately take its toll and adversely impact the team's performance as well as the desired outcome. As we saw in Chapter 8, a lack of skills within the team will create anxiety, while a lack of resources results in frustration (Knoster et al. 2000), both of which adversely impact the desired outcome.

As a team leader and supervisor it is essential, in your desire to build an effective team, to consider the level of training and the type of tools necessary to ensure the team's success. All nonprofit organizations are concerned with managing limited resources, being frugal with entrusted resources, and therefore hitting the sweet spot, one that achieves a balance between what is needed and what is ultimately available, is extremely important.

To achieve this one has to fully assess the current context. It is important as a part of this assessment to have clear communication about what is expected and what tools as well as what skills will be needed to ensure success. In my own organizational practice, I want to hear from my team members about their perspective and I need to expand the information gathering to include outside experts as well as others who have managed through a similar situation. Feedback and communication from multiple sources will help you to determine the types of tools that will be required as well as the training that will be needed. Tools, I should note, come in many forms and can be as tangible as capital equipment and as intangible as a tweaking of existing policy in order to ensure that barriers are reduced. Training, too, can be formal and conducted by external sources, or informal, such as when employees are afforded time to familiarize themselves with the new tools. Once you have fully assessed the current situation, you will be better able to provide the team with resources to ensure their success.

My nonprofit's experience with the recent pandemic serves as an example. We were faced with a decision point with regard to our in-home counseling services. Do we simply put services on hold until the pandemic passes, or do we move forward with purchasing the equipment and providing the training necessary to continue our service delivery using telehealth? The budget did not include funds for the computers and equipment needed for remote work or funds for additional training, nor did it include the cost of additional network access and software to ensure connectivity between our in-home therapists and the people we serve. Because the pandemic necessitated that we no longer meet face-to-face we were confronted with a significant decision. As a team, despite concerns about limited resources, we decided to pursue the tools and training necessary to ensure that our services continued. As a result, we pivoted quickly, developed policies for telecommuting, secured internet connectivity for clients and staff, purchased the equipment needed, and provided the training necessary to have our entire in-home services division move to telehealth. Ultimately, we were quite successful and, to our surprise, we were able to generate additional revenue through higher utilization for our in-home counseling services, which in turn covered the added cost of equipment and training. Our success, though, was clearly centered around ensuring that the team had the right tools and the right training to execute the identified goals and objectives.

Build the Team's Culture

As we know from Chapter 4, a strong organizational culture is key to the success of the agency. This is true as well for your team. You can use a number of the strategies identified in Chapter 4 to build a mission- and vision-focused team that shares in the values and beliefs of the organization as seen through the way in which the team works together. You can also strengthen your team's culture by creating an operationalized mission and vision statement for the team. As we discussed, a mission statement describes the purpose of the organization while a vision statement describes what the organization hopes to be. This is true for a mission and vision statement that is operationalized at the team level. Within my nonprofit the mission statement for my senior leadership team is *to advance the mission of the agency through leadership, inspiration, and support*, while the vision statement is *advancing the agency's mission together through a trusting, cohesive, and committed team*. As you can see, the team's mission and vision statement connect directly to the agency's larger mission statement while helping to define the work of the senior leadership team.

Developing the operationalized mission and vision statement had as much value as the statements themselves. As is often the case, process is extremely important. Given this, when a mission and vision statement is developed by the team it becomes an opportunity to help with value clarification, help underscore what is important to the team, and ensure that everyone is heard in the process. In the end the team shares a greater understanding of what is important to each individual as well as what is central to the successful working of the team.

Once developed the team mission and vision statement becomes a point of reference for how the team works together going forward. In our case we regularly ask ourselves as well as each other about our fidelity to the mission and vision statement. Are we, for example, working together in a way that engenders trust? Are we committed as a team and are we cohesive in our efforts together? Something as simple as a short discussion in response to any one of these questions helps the team to recalibrate and move forward more successfully.

Another critical aspect of your team's culture is its capacity to exist as a learning environment. As a manager and a leader, you have a central responsibility to ensure that team members have opportunities to learn and grow. Opportunities for learning and growth can be formal or informal. Trainings and seminars fall into the category of formal learning opportunities while informal opportunities can be something as simple as consistent encouragement for personal and professional development. Asking a team member to present something that they are currently learning, for example, to the larger team helps to create a premium on the learning process. In your leadership practice, strive to encourage people to develop to their full potential, even if this means that they may ultimately decide to learn and grow into an area that is outside the work of the organization. Better to encourage growth and reap the benefit of a learning environment than try to hold people back because you fear losing them.

Inextricably connected to the creation of a learning environment is the importance of ensuring that your leadership practice includes what I call the *forgiveness factor*. If people are truly going to learn and grow, it goes without saying that there will be missteps and mistakes. If you are learning, you are not an expert, and even if you are an expert, something can go wrong. The literature in this area is quite interesting. For example, in organizations where forgiveness is present employees are more likely to go above and beyond in their work for the agency (see, e.g., Radulovic, Thomas, Epitropaki, & Legood, 2019).

In my own career I recall making a mistake or two and if it were not for my supervisor's willingness to forgive me, I certainly wouldn't be here today. Of course, forgiveness is closely connected to the transgressor's humility and willingness to learn and thereby avoid repeating the mistake. As a supervisor and leader, you are largely responsible for setting the tone for whether or not people are able to make a mistake, take responsibility for their error, and then take the steps necessary to learn and grow. Be sure to create a space for this learning to occur through your supervisory meetings, team meetings, and your own behavior. I will, for example, let people know when I have made a mistake and what I have done to address it. This creates the ability to role model how mistakes will happen and what it looks like when someone takes responsibility for their error.

Connected to this is what I refer to as the affective side of team management. Our work in the nonprofit world is particularly intense, and as a result we are typically dealing with many feelings as we work to advance the organization's mission. Because of this it is not uncommon for team members to feel emotionally charged with a given topic. Leadership sometimes runs from the feeling side of our employees' experience. This is in part because we are taught to focus on the left brain, logical, plan-based activities of organizational life within Western culture. It also happens because as a leader you are worried that things will come unraveled and that they might get out of control.

Let me suggest that instead of avoiding this, you pursue your practice perspective of being antigravitational. Move toward the affect that is presented to you and create a space to allow your team member and employee share what they are feeling. The impact is quite remarkable. First the employee feels a sense of relief that they have been heard. This is followed by a feeling that the precipitating situation, whatever it was, is now somehow more manageable, and also that the team members feel a sense of safety and trust that makes it possible for them to move forward.

Interestingly, managing the affective side of leadership within my own practice has resulted in my team members dubbing one seat in my office as the "crying chair." It is not that I make people come in and cry, it is that when people are feeling emotionally charged they have realized that it's safe to share what they feel and have even come into my office saying that they need to "sit in the crying chair." While they say this in a lighthearted way it is also a signal that they have something heavy to share and it is emblematic of the permission they have to share how they are feeling.

While I am encouraging you to move toward the feelings that your team members may be experiencing and allow them to express themselves, I also want to encourage you to pursue your own affect experience in a thoughtful way. It is important that you display a level of emotional intelligence that shows maturity when it comes to dealing with employees as well as situations within your team. If you fly off the handle, are quick to anger, and are inconsiderate of your team members, you will undoubtedly do considerable harm to the entire team and negatively impact your ability to be an effective leader.

Ultimately your goal as a leader within your team is to create a win-win scenario. When this happens, the organization reaps the benefits of the team members' good work and the team members feel that they are treated and paid fairly for the work that they are expected to do. Maintaining a win-win posture makes it possible for you to carefully consider the alignment between what the agency needs and what the employee needs. When these things are not aligned then it is safe to say that an adjustment may be in order. Sometimes the adjustment takes the form of new or different responsibilities for the employee, and other times it might take the form of problem solving with regard to schedules and existing duties. In all cases the goal is to achieve a balance where each party can experience the relationship as one that works. Of course, the key is that our service is always to the mission of the organization, and so if a win-win cannot be achieved with this in mind, it may well be time for the team member to get off the proverbial bus at the next stop.

Maintaining a win-win balanced-scorecard perspective makes it possible to take the affect out of this aspect of the employees' work situation. If the work situation is not a win-win, then it's fine for the team member to move on and in fact it is something that you'd want as an expectation when someone feels that they aren't getting what they need within their work environment. Interestingly, holding this stance with team members has made it possible for former employees within my organization to return at a later date to another position. Together we joke that they went on sabbatical (unpaid, of course) and have returned to fulfill a new role within the organization. Be sure to work with your team members in a way that helps them to see how important it is for everyone to feel that the arrangement is both fair and responsible as the team works in service of the mission.

Celebrate and Recognize the Right People

Another strategy that will help to build your team centers around the important idea of taking the time necessary to recognize team members who are performing in a way that supports the overall work of the organization. Taking time to recognize people for efforts that align with your organization's vision, mission, values, and beliefs sends an important message not only to the individual being recognized, but also to the entire team. As we discuss in Chapter 6, recognizing and incentivizing mission-focused behavior goes a long way toward building strong cultural norms as well as affective organizational commitment. It is also important to create opportunities to celebrate the entire team for their hard work and for the team's overall accomplishments. Celebrating the entire team helps to ensure that everyone feels a part of what has been accomplished.

Of course, there are innumerable ways to celebrate and recognize your team members. Some forms of recognition are as simple as sending along a congratulatory email or note to a team member, or including a shout-out during a staff meeting. More formal systems for recognition and celebration, as we discuss in Chapter 7 (see System

5: Retreats and Events) include employee awards, annual conferences, and ceremonies. The best strategies in this area are typically a
combination of both informal and formal systems to help recognize
and celebrate the individuals as well as the larger team.

An example of an informal as well as a formal strategy that we
use in my nonprofit is to celebrate employee anniversaries. I write a
personal letter to each employee on their anniversary of joining the
team. Then in the month of their anniversary they are celebrated at
their respective staff meeting, when team members take a moment to
informally thank the individual for their contribution. This involves
team members sharing how they feel the person has contributed to
the team and thanking them for all their hard work. This serves to
underscore the individual's contribution to the agency. And then
finally there's a formal recognition program in which the employee
receives a gift card for specific years of service—5, 10, 15 years, and
so on. Taken together, these three strategies help to solidify the role
that the individual plays within the team and in our efforts to achieve
the organization's mission.

A successful team and successful teams throughout the entire
organization serve as the secret sauce for your organization's ability
to realize its mission. Your ability to lead, your skills as a supervisor,
and the capacity for your team to accomplish what it sets out to do is
at the heart of your nonprofit's ability to fulfill its mission. The strategies explored in this chapter, when pursued in the context of the
earlier chapters in this book, provide you with specific capabilities
to ensure success. Do not give away the opportunity to capitalize on
these strategies. Work to be aware of your own leadership style, help
your team to build their open quadrant while building a strong team
culture, and your success will be assured.

11

Strategic Alliances

UP TO THIS point we have spent time together thinking about strategies for developing your skills as a nonprofit leader, ways in which to help your employees and your team develop, as well as strategies for building systems and organizational culture that will help to achieve your agency's mission. Much of the discourse at this point has been inward-focused, which is quite appropriate given the magnitude of what needs to be mastered in order to be effective as a nonprofit manager and leader. We turn now in a purposeful way to a more external lens on nonprofit leadership and management to explore the important topic area of strategic alliances.

A strategic alliance is any agreement between two or more organizations that is designed to help strengthen each party. Alliances, as we will discuss, cover the gamut from informal shared collaborative efforts to highly structured and legally executed agreements. As a nonprofit leader it is important for you to first understand the various forms of strategic alliance that are present and then develop the skills necessary to optimize the use of alliances to support and advance the mission of your nonprofit organization.

In my more than four decades of experience in nonprofit leadership and management, I have seen the good, the bad, and the ugly when it comes to nonprofit strategic alliances. Given this, I share my experience, where the bumps have been encountered as well as what worked particularly well, in the hope that you can avoid some of the pitfalls I have experienced as well as leverage the positive experiences.

Types of Strategic Alliances

Let us start by describing the various types of strategic alliances that are present within the nonprofit world. The forms of strategic alliance that follow are not meant to be all encompassing, but rather a fair representation of what you will encounter as you work to build relationships that can help advance the mission of your organization. As we move through the list you will see that each form of strategic alliance involves a progressively more formal structure. At the core of any strategic alliance is the question of autonomy versus integration. The less formal the strategic alliance, the less the integration will be required, and the more autonomy will be found between the respective entities. Conversely, the more formal the strategic alliance, the more integration is present, and, along with this, the less autonomy the entities will experience.

The question of integration and autonomy is an important consideration when thinking about how a strategic alliance might benefit your organization. It is important to understand that an agreement that results in a high degree of integration will ultimately impact the amount of autonomy that your organization has. Autonomy is critical because it speaks to the very core of your organization's existence. An autonomous organization has a board of directors that can chart its own course forward, is able to make its own decisions regarding strategic priorities, and can pursue the development and use of resources without the constraints that exist when your agency is highly integrated with another. On the other hand, some organizations end up needing strategic alliances that involve a high degree of integration to survive. The key is to understand the implications of agreements and how they impact these two factors.

Associations

No matter the area of nonprofit work you're involved in, you'll find that there is a plethora of associations related to your organization's work. In my own organization we belong to no fewer than six associations, all related to the work that the organization does. Associations are found at the national, state, and regional level and are typically concerned with a specific aspect of nonprofit work. There are nonprofit associations that are concerned with advancing the work of the nonprofit industry for a state or, depending on their focus, on a national basis. Then there are associations that are specific to a particular niche of nonprofit work. For example, my nonprofit belongs to, at a national level, the Child Welfare League of America and the National Council for Behavioral Health, and at a local level the Alliance for Substance Abuse and Mental Health Services. Each of these respective groups works to help advance their members' practice within their area of focus and interest.

Members can benefit from training, conferences, support with legislative priorities, group purchasing on items such as electronic health records, insurance coverage, and the like. The level of integration within associations is typically quite low and as a result the autonomy that exists between the various membership organizations remains very high. Often the work that is accomplished within the association context, while important, can be considered "low-hanging fruit." Said another way, the initiatives do not require any of the entities to reach too far or require too much effort on the part of any of the member organizations.

As someone who has been on the board and has had a member seat on many different associations over the years, I have always found it fascinating to watch a group work through a given priority. Once it gets to the point where one organization's autonomy might be adversely impacted, then just watch how quickly things begin to fall apart. Recall my friend from the North Country of New Hampshire who does not mind change, so long as it doesn't matter! This is a similar situation. In strategic alliances where there is limited integration, pursuing more integrated tasks becomes arduous if not impossible.

This is not to say that associations do not have their value. To the contrary, they can be extremely helpful. Consider, for example, the limits placed on nonprofit organizations in their ability to lobby in the legislative process. Associations often can serve as a vehicle for pursuing important legislative initiatives in a way that protects the nonprofit's tax-exempt status. The point, however, is to understand that efforts within associations that require a higher degree of integration generally fall short of their desired goal. Best to work in your role as a nonprofit leader to help your organization benefit from the low-hanging fruit that the association can easily provide.

Interagency Collaboration

As we move through the strategic alliance continuum we come to interagency collaboration. Interagency collaboration within the nonprofit industry can take multiple forms and can be formal as well as informal. Consider, for example, a nonprofit organization that provides a meeting space for another nonprofit organization. In one example we operated a parent aide program that provided supervised visitation services for court-involved parents. In some instances, there was a history of violence on the part of one of the parents and so in-home supervised visits were not only unwise but strictly forbidden by the court. In this instance the local family resource center would provide a meeting space for our team members. This interagency collaboration helped both organizations by advancing each agency's respective mission. The family resource center was helping families without having to pay for the personnel (we covered that element) and we benefited because we had the ability to provide a supervised visit without paying for space (paid for by the family resource center). In this instance the arrangement was informal and set up with a simple phone call between the organizations' respective leadership teams. This would be an example of a collaborative strategic alliance that falls under the use of *shared resources*.

Related to this is the collaborative strategic alliance of in-kind services. In-kind services represent the dedication of a tangible resource or service to the work of two respective organizations. One example that comes to mind is the donation of housing we receive for a transitional housing service for individuals with serious and persistent mental illness. In this instance the use of the residences is provided without rental cost to the organization. The complexity, as you might imagine, becomes greater as these types of strategic alliances are realized. For example, the use of the properties involves a contractual agreement with performance requirements for maintenance and upkeep of the facilities. The organization that provides the housing maintains ownership of the residences and my organization ensures the upkeep of the sites. As you can see there is a bit more integration here and autonomy is slightly ratcheted down in terms of what we can do with the use of the in-kind asset.

Contractual service agreements represent one of the more formal forms of interagency collaboration. In this instance each organization remains autonomous, with the exception of the service delivery elements described within the contractual service agreement. An example that comes to mind involves a small nonprofit housing organization that desired to have a case management capability to serve the individuals within their housing services. In this instance, they were not large enough to afford the electronic health record required by the state, nor did the rules allow for them to operate case management services, as this was delegated to the designated managed care entity for the region. The designated managed care entity, it turns out, was extremely interested in finding a better way to serve this specialized population, and so they agreed to subcontract the case management services to the housing agency.

This ultimately was a win-win for both organizations. The designated managed care entity met service delivery goals for a specialized population and the housing agency now had the ability to provide an important service directly to the people they serve. As we have pointed out, the arrangement required even more integration and less autonomy on the part of the housing organization. As a result of the subcontract, the housing agency had to perform in accordance with the regional managed care entity's service delivery, reporting, and documentation standards, as well as work within the confines of the rate provided them. The key here is to enter into agreements with your eyes wide open and ensure that the loss of autonomy and the increase in integration remains aligned with the vision and mission of your nonprofit organization.

Networks

Networks represent the next step along the continuum of strategic alliances. In a network arrangement two or more organizations come together to develop a formal structure in pursuit of specific services or deliverables. Often networks involve the creation of a separate legal entity, such as a limited liability corporation (LLC), which becomes the formal structure for the pursuit of the goals that are shared between the respective entities. The member organizations have rights and responsibilities related to the operation of the network and, as you can imagine, integration is high in the areas affected by the enterprise and autonomy is reduced accordingly.

My nonprofit, over the course of my tenure, has belonged to several networks. When managed care first arrived, for example, a broad array of behavioral and physical health organizations joined together for the purpose of contracting with insurers to provide a system of care for people within the region. This was an LLC that ultimately hired a management team that in turn contracted with member organizations to provide an array of services. Similarly, we belonged to a system of care networks that came together to formally contract to provide child welfare services to the families in the state with the greatest level of need. In both instances our membership responsibilities were highly defined and governance for each network was fully developed, ensuring that member organizations had a voice and integration between the respective organizations was high.

As an organization, our membership meant that we gave up autonomy in several areas, such as certain service delivery policies and billing practices, but the trade-off was better than the potential adverse impact if we did not join the network. In one instance, for example, if you were not in the network, you were unable to contract with the Department of Health and Human Services for service delivery. Networks like any type of strategic alliance come with a certain level of benefit as well as a varying degree of costs. The key from a leadership perspective is to fully understand the impact the required integration will have on your organization and whether the costs associated with the alliance are outweighed by the benefits.

I discuss elements to consider when considering strategic alliances, including becoming a part of a network, in greater detail in the following sections.

Mergers

Mergers represent one more step on the road to full integration. Mergers within the nonprofit world can be quite complex and require the involvement of legal advice and, oftentimes, government oversight. Your organization's tax-exempt status is granted by the federal government and it is important to ensure that your plan to merge with another organization won't threaten this important legal standing. In addition, many nonprofits have property that is placed into service with the use of covenants to satisfy the funding source. HUD funds, for example, while extremely beneficial for the organization, have requirements for property that is placed into use that will have to be fully addressed in the transfer of the given property.

Often nonprofit organizations pursue mergers when they perceive a financial benefit to the combining of shared efforts. For example, two human resource departments become one, IT departments, business offices, and other backroom functions merge, and executive leadership teams are consolidated. At the front of the house services might be consolidated as well. For example, two case management services become a single service working to meet the organization's mission. In other instances, the newly merged organization might find themselves in the position to expand their complementary service array. An agency with case management services might merge with an organization that provides community-based residential services. When this happens the newly merged entity now has a larger share of the service delivery array for a given area or population.

Mergers are complex for many reasons beyond the legal elements mentioned earlier. Many questions must be explored in depth. The new entity must decide how the new board of directors will be formed. There are many layers to ironing out the governance questions. The new entity must decide who the new board president will be, as well as the role that each of the former board members will play. Will they all come along or will some members of the respective boards step down? There are similar questions for agency leadership and management. The questions that have to be answered are many and varied, from the organization's name to the policies (human resource, program, and business) that will ultimately be adopted to guide the new entity.

As you can see, mergers require a great deal of effort on the part of agency leadership and are not to be taken lightly. Because of the complexity associated with mergers it is not uncommon to see that a driving force behind a merger between two organizations is the question of organizational survival. In other instances, there are significant factors that heighten the strategic benefit that can come from a merger. Usually there are forces in the operating environment that are impacting each organization, which in turn heighten the desirability of a merger between the entities.

As you can imagine, mergers end up significantly impacting the autonomy of both entities and result in a high degree of integration. As a leader of an organization heading toward a merger, your work will be to ensure that there is a balanced approach to integration and to the loss of autonomy. Working to ensure that the result is equitable and can stand up to scrutiny from internal as well as external stakeholders is extremely important. You do not want to be in a position where the merger ends up hurting your organization's ability to achieve its mission and vision. The goal, of course, is to create a win-win situation for both entities.

Acquisitions

Acquisitions represent yet one more type of strategic alliance. An acquisition, simply stated, is when one organization acquires another. In the world of nonprofit organizations, acquisitions occur when one organization gives over its assets, operations, and governance to another organization. When money changes hands there are multiple legal requirements that have to be managed and for 501(c)3s the assets must be used for charitable purposes. Oftentimes, when the acquisition is done, to make it possible for the nonprofit being acquired to continue its mission the assets are simply passed over to the agency that is acquiring them. This is true of the liabilities as well.

Within my nonprofit organization we have acquired two other organizations. These were smaller entities that were struggling with the changes that were occurring in the system of care for children's services. In both examples we pursued an asset donation strategy rather than a more complex and legally costly acquisition strategy. The end result was the same, as both organizations became a part of our overall agency operations.

For the organization being acquired, the acquisition itself means that the entity's autonomy is no longer present. There are ways to help ensure that the work continues beyond the existence of the entity, and this can be done through the legal documents that the respective organizations draw up. But, to be clear, the board of directors, the leadership, and the employees are no longer part of the agency being acquired. Boards typically disband and employment for those who stay on is with the agency that did the acquiring.

Key Points

Strategic alliances play an important role in your organization's success and your ability to understand as well as manage and leverage the benefits of various forms of alliance is critical. As we have seen, the questions of autonomy and integration are important considerations as you work to determine which alliance strategies work best for your agency. There are a few other points, as well, that merit exploration and should be considered, no matter which type of strategic alliance you pursue.

Mission and Vision Alignment

First, as you think about whether to pursue a strategic alliance, whether it is in the form of an association or far down on the continuum in the form of a merger or acquisition, you will want to ensure that there is a full alignment between the mission and vision of your organization and that of the entity you intend to form an alliance with. If the respective organization's mission and vision are not aligned, then don't pursue an alliance. Find another partner, or rethink the plan altogether, but don't, I mean *don't*, pursue the strategic alliance. This is true no matter how attractive the opportunity looks and no matter how capable you feel you are of managing through this type of difference.

The question of alignment in this area becomes increasingly important in light of the fact that any alliance will require that your organization begin to cede autonomy and will have to engage in integration. When the mission and vision are not aligned, it will not take long before you and your internal stakeholders will suddenly realize that this change does matter and that you don't like it, no, you don't like it at all! If you have taken steps toward a strategic alliance, it may be that you have gone too far and the damage to you and your organization can be significant.

Avoiding Mission Drift

In a like way, it is important to be careful not to accept seemingly minor differences in organizational mission. It may be that the potential alliance promises so many apparent benefits that you feel that a few elements of mission that are not aligned would be fine. You might find yourself conducting a cost-benefit analysis and deciding, along with your internal team, that you could live with the differences. Be careful here as you may find yourself compromising in a way that will create a mission-drift situation. Remember, one degree of separation at the start of a journey seems meaningless. Consider what happens one mile down the road as the paths become significantly separate. Avoid compromising when it comes to the foundational values that are part and parcel of your organization's mission.

I recall the experience of a colleague of mine who ended up in an acquisition in which their organization was purchased by a for-profit company. Everything seemed beautifully aligned. The one difference, of course, was the presence of shareholders in the for-profit, and as a result, the requirement that the services and programs of the organization return a profit. This one difference, one that seemed inconsequential at the start of the arrangement, became untenable as time passed and services were dismantled based on their level of profitability.

Given this, hold fast and know that something that seems small and manageable on the front end can become significant as time goes on. It is better to find another partner with a stronger mission and vision alignment or even an altogether different path forward.

Culture

As you work to implement strategic alliances, consider the alignment between the respective organizations' cultures. Organizational culture is omnipresent and plays a significant role in the success of any strategic endeavor. As we noted in Chapter 4, Peter Drucker, the famous management guru, is attributed with saying that "culture eats strategy for breakfast." What he means by this is the reality that if your cultures aren't aligned and in support of the alliance you envision, then you can, in the word of Donnie Brasco, "Fuhgeddaboudit!" There is no way to be successful in an alliance that hopes to pursue a high degree of integration without addressing and successfully navigating the normative cultures that exist within the respective entities.

Culture is less of a concern when the level of integration is lower. So, you can, for example, engage in strategic alliances with associations and not have a perfectly aligned culture between the respective member organizations, but as you move along the continuum of strategic alliances, you will need to carefully consider the culture that exists.

My recommendation to you in this area is to avail yourself of this book's fourth chapter and leverage the strategies identified there to work toward positively impacting the culture. Be careful, though, as culture change requires significant heavy lifting and I personally know many leaders who found the marriage of two incompatible cultures to be not only challenging but sadly insurmountable in their effort to achieve a strategic alliance that incorporates a high degree of integration.

Short-Term Gain, Long-Term Pain

As you move toward various forms of strategic alliance, you will be tempted to look at the immediate benefits without considering the long-term impact. Rather than follow this path, put the leadership practice perspectives found in Chapter 2 to work for you. For example, always take the long view. Situations will arise that will heighten the level of urgency that is present. No doubt you will need to respond when this happens, but instead of just responding, take time to consider the desired state, how you hope the organization will be in the long term, and then make sure that your action in the moment is one that supports the long view.

Similarly, be antigravitational as needed. You do not need to go with the flow. In fact, it might benefit you to take a step back and move in the opposite direction. Of course, all of this requires that you continue to build your own self-awareness as well as your team's ability to be more fully aware.

Leveraging the leadership practice perspectives will help you avoid taking on a path that appears helpful in the short term, but ultimately ends up creating long-term pain for you and for your organization.

Staying Ahead of the Curve

Another key point related to the various forms of strategic alliance is to practice your leadership in a way that ensures that you regularly watch for opportunities that might arise that could benefit your organization. Be active with outside associations. Volunteer, offer to be on a committee, join a board of directors, and engage in other activities that will help you to be aware of what the possibilities are. In addition, being fully engaged helps outside stakeholders to become aware of your organization, as well as your role within the agency.

Remember the fourth leadership practice perspective suggests that you leverage serendipity. Become the individual upon which luck will grace itself. Serendipity only visits the prepared mind. Take steps to ensure that you are prepared to leverage the strategic alliance possibilities that arise.

Understanding the various forms of strategic alliances and the key points related to ensure their successful implementation provides you with yet another tool to help advance the work of your nonprofit organization. Leveraging this knowledge can help to create possibilities for your agency as well as solutions for challenges that you may encounter.

My work with associations has yielded benefits for my organization's work in the behavioral health field by ensuring that new legislation is passed to improve the system of care. We have also been able to expand our footprint in service delivery while helping smaller organizations to continue their missions through the acquisition of their services. In one instance, the smaller organization was unable to weather the rate-setting challenges and risked losing everything. Because of our size we were able to step in and thereby keep a critically important service in place while we worked to correct the rate structure.

Whether through becoming a part of an association or working at the other end of the continuum, strategic alliances represent an opportunity to benefit your organization's ability to achieve its mission. As a nonprofit leader, working successfully in this realm can become an important part of your leadership practice toolbox.

12

From Theory to Practice: Bringing It All Together

THE STRATEGIES WE have explored throughout this book are strategies that I have employed throughout my career as a nonprofit leader and manager. They are strategies I have learned from my studies and research within the field, from my mentors along the way, as well as from trial and error as I worked to develop my own leadership capability. Now more than 40 years into my leadership practice I can say with surety that the road we travel to become effective nonprofit leaders is truly a journey. Even now I continue to realize how much more there is to learn in my quest to be the best leader possible. Throughout this journey I have tried to treat each experience, encounter, and challenge as an opportunity to develop my skills and build upon the toolbox that helps to ensure successful leadership and management.

The strategies explored throughout this book come together to provide you with a framework that supports your leadership success. It is not enough to think about your individual leadership style and techniques. While efforts to develop your individual capabilities are extremely important, your ability to lead effectively exists simultaneously within the multiple levels explored in this book. Building an effective team and impacting the organizational culture are but two additional areas that require mastery in order to ensure your leadership efficacy. As you develop your ability to be effective in these areas as well as the other areas explored, you leverage your ability to be effective as a nonprofit leader and manager.

Throughout our time together I have tried to provide you with practical strategies that will support your efforts within each of the various strategies that form the framework for success. Starting first with the question of your individual leadership capabilities, it is wise to focus on developing your personal skills. Strive to incorporate the practice perspectives we explored in Chapter 2. Some of the practice perspectives will come to you more easily than others. Take heart, though, and work to move your practice perspectives forward. I can recall in my own development, for example, how hard it was to move toward the practice perspective that would ensure my leadership efforts took the long view. I was impatient and wanted to get to the destination. In time, though, I realized that stepping back and letting go of the need for immediacy opened a whole set of possibilities that were heretofore unavailable to me. Moving further into this practice perspective also played an important role in helping me to better manage the inner pressure that I felt (the seventh practice perspective). I suspect that you, too, will find that the various practice perspectives inform each other and those that come more easily to you will help to advance your efforts in the other practice perspectives.

As you work to build your individual leadership skills, leverage the leadership development strategies that are also explored in Chapter 2. Watch for the opportunities for leadership development as well as the opportunities to engage within your organization's many efforts. Before long, you will not only have expanded your own leadership toolbox but will also have come to the attention of other leaders within the organization. I recall, for example, being an entry-level program director in an organization that was growing by leaps and bounds. At every turn I offered to become involved and support the organization's efforts. It was not long before I was involved in so many initiatives that the executive director recommended to the senior leadership team that I join their weekly management meetings to report on the efforts I was involved in. Soon I was asked to accept a new role within the senior leadership team. Availing myself of opportunities helped me to develop my skills in a wide array of areas and ultimately helped to ensure that senior leadership began to look at me in a different light. Perhaps, they thought, Paul could take on some additional responsibilities and a new role.

As we discuss in Chapter 3, it is important to consider what type of leader you hope to be. Choosing a leadership style becomes an important part of the overall framework for success. Throughout the chapter we took a high-altitude review of seven leadership styles that might appeal to your own sensibility when it comes to leadership practice. Servant leadership is explored in greater depth in this chapter. Recall that there is a tool found in the Appendix that can help you to consider your personal assets when it comes to the 10 characteristics that are central to the model. I recommend that you avail yourself of this tool and consider strategies that you might use to enhance your capabilities within this leadership approach. Using the tool in an interactive way with other team members also helps to advance an important exploration of the 10 characteristics among and between team members. Talking about how members of the team listen to each other, for example, can open a door to improving leadership practice at multiple levels.

We also explored a traditional leadership and managerial approach for considering leadership behavior, given the context of your organization's and team's capabilities. The Tannenbaum and Schmidt (1973) model is extremely helpful when it comes to considering how decisions are made within your leadership practice. When you fully appreciate the context in which decisions are made and can move successfully between telling, selling, consulting, and joining, your team will come to appreciate the clarity of your leadership practice. In contrast, if you are not clear about the variables and the dynamics present and do not move successfully between each of the four strategies, the road ahead can be a rough one.

The work involved to develop your personal leadership skills, as we have noted, is a journey and one that will take time. In fact, the journey should last throughout your professional career. Simultaneously, it makes sense to utilize strategies to leverage the strength that organizational culture can provide to ensure success. I can say with surety that your success as a leader is inextricably tied to the culture found within your team and within your organization. *Culture happens* and if you are not aware of its impact and the strategies available to leverage positive culture, then you are missing a significant element in your effort to be a successful nonprofit leader and manager. Make use of the strategies we discuss in Chapter 4.

The strategies provided in Chapter 4 become an important part of a framework for success. Pursue each strategy fully to ensure the success of your organization's normative culture. As we have discussed it is essential that your organization's culture work to support you and your team's leadership practice. A true example of simplexity, the strategies to ensure success in the creation of positive organizational culture are so straightforward and simple that they seem elementary. Conversely, there is a great deal of complexity involved in changing an organization's culture. Creating meaningful opportunities for belonging; leveraging the factors that shape norms; and understanding the relationship between vision, mission, values, beliefs, and behavior all provide a window to ensure your success within this frame. However, you must ensure that you are clearly situated within your practice perspectives and intentional in your efforts to ensure that the type of culture you shape is the type of culture that you desire. Sometimes a simple act can have a significant impact, helping to move you in the right direction, and at the same time the investment of considerable time and effort could have just the opposite effect on the organization's culture—despite your best efforts.

I recall a time, for example, when I was asked to step in and run a community residence for young people because the program director had lost all credibility and was loathed and mistrusted. This individual, right or wrong, was seen as someone who was aloof from the team and a leader who held himself to a different standard than the rest of the employees. He ruled with an iron fist and took limited joy in anything that anyone did; in fact, he generally disapproved of any effort that he had not initiated. I knew something about his history with the team and was working hard to change the norms, or unspoken patterns of behavior, that had developed. I wanted to show the team that I was a different type of leader. One day, not long after my arrival as the interim program director, I pulled into the parking lot and as I got out of the car I heard a huge commotion going on within the house—lots of running about, yelling, and laughter. As I came toward the house things suddenly quieted down. Odd, I thought, I wonder what is going on? As soon as I came in the front door, I found out . . . all eight residents and the four staff on duty were standing in the front hall, each with a bucket of water which they handily threw on me as I opened door and stepped inside. I was drenched to the bone and, to say the least, quite startled. I also knew that I was at a decision point and my response to this surprise attack would shape my relationship with the team going forward. So, I decided to be antigravitational and respond by laughing, taking hold of one of the buckets and joining in the water fight. It was a small act in a moment of time that ultimately became a story told time and again: a story that solidified that I was a different type of leader, a leader who was serious, yet able to have fun. A leader who could roll with the punches as well as be part of the group, while at the same time be entrusted to move the program forward.

Shaping organizational culture is conceptually simple, yet operationally complex. Take time to use what we have explored in order to truly work to advance the organization's normative culture. Similarly, working to cue up your team for generative leadership capability as identified in Chapter 5 will also help you in your efforts to be an effective leader. Creating opportunities for leadership, supporting the ability for people to trust each other, take risks, develop their leadership attributes, practice communication and feedback, as well as working to enhance all the other elements of the generative leadership frame will help your organization to be a true powerhouse. Imagine having a team of mission- and vision-focused, affectively committed employees who have the ability to step up and take on leadership responsibilities. A generative leadership approach will help you to achieve this. Organizations that have increased their ability to support generative leadership are organizations that excel during the normal course of events and thrive in difficult times in their efforts to realize their agency's mission and vision for the future.

Recall that the Appendix includes an assessment tool that will help you to gauge the presence of the six core elements and seven subthemes related to the creation of generative leadership practice within your organization. The tool is designed to assess for each of the elements at the individual, team, and organizational frame and presents an opportunity for you to consider strategies to advance you and your team as well as your organization's capacity in each of the core elements and subthemes. Take advantage of this tool and, if you do, you will find that by identifying and then implementing strategies to heighten the presence of each theme, you will enhance the ability of your agency at each of the three frames to engender effective nonprofit leadership.

Similarly, Chapter 6 provides a window into strategies to enhance your employees' engagement and performance management. As noted within the chapter the Appendix contains a particularly helpful tool for assessing your strengths in employee performance management. We know from the literature (see, e.g., Wolf & Zwick, 2008 or Phipps & Ndjnguri, 2013) and from our own lived managerial and leadership experience, that a well-engaged employee is an employee who will go the extra mile to ensure the success of the organization. The tool makes it possible to develop a better understanding of our strengths in this area, as well as areas for growth and development. Each element that is assessed using the tool represents an opportunity for leveraging your team's capacity to fulfill the organization's mission. It also represents an opportunity for you to engage in some self-reflection about your own leadership and managerial efforts in this area. This is an important element of growing your leadership practice perspective of awareness as well as your leadership development strategy, identified as *sharpening your saw*.

I was surprised once we put this tool to use to see how many leaders discovered a differential assessment of their behavior when they considered each of their employees individually. In one instance a leader exclaimed how surprised he was that he regularly set goals for some employees while avoiding this practice with others. Since we know that goal setting is an important element of employee engagement and performance management, it stands to reason that it would make sense to ensure that this happens for all employees. In this instance, as in other instances, the tool helped the leader rethink why he had fallen into a pattern of avoiding goal-setting with some employees and not others, and then commit himself to refining his practice to ensure that all employees received the benefit of this practice.

Performance management continues to help us build a framework for success through the exploration of strategies to engage and support the effectiveness of employees through a deeper dive into what is known about effective supervision practices. Strong supervision practices translate into effective and more affectively committed employees. Following best practices with fidelity will not only help you achieve desired goals and objectives at an individual, team, and organizational level, it will also help you develop, train, and retain the best team members. In my experience there are generally four primary reasons why people leave one position and take another. The most obvious one is money, which we know is not something the nonprofit sector can always do something about. The other reasons, though, are ones that we can impact, and next in line after pay is the employee's supervisor. People leave their jobs because they cannot stand their boss! This of course underscores the importance of developing your supervisory practice, along with your managerial and leadership-based skills, so that you'll be able to help keep good employees.

In Chapter 7 we explore strategies that help to ensure the development of successful systems in support of a framework for success. Remember, if you do not develop sound systems within the organization, you will find yourself dependent on individual personalities. We all know great people, and likely you are one of them. Great people can and will do great things, but their ability to impact an organization in the quest to realize its vision and mission will be wholly enhanced by the presence of thoughtfully laid-out systems. Similarly, individuals who are not in the "great" category generally need thoughtfully developed and implemented systems in order to ensure their success. With the right systems supporting them, many employees can themselves become "great people."

The principles laid out in Chapter 7 provide a measure for you to consider the efficacy of any given system. Remember, as we have discussed, all work within the nonprofit must emulate and build up from the mission. In order to make sure you are on the right track, use the principles shared within the chapter to double-check as well as refine the systems that you build. In support of this, the Appendix contains a tool that can help you consider each system within the organization and how it helps or misses the mark on realizing the important principles for effective systems.

Chapter 7 also includes some specific systems that you might decide to model in support of your organization and your leadership practice. System development is critical and complex. By following the principles we have identified, and the core systems explored, I believe you will experience a considerable amount of success. Of course, none of the systems we explore exist in a vacuum. Your ability to build on your leadership practice, the presence of generative leadership within your team, a positive organizational culture, and effective employee engagement help to set the course for ensuring the success of the system you intend to operationalize.

In an organization where employees feel disenfranchised, for example, they are not likely to wholeheartedly participate in a communication practice that is direct and intentional. Similarly, employees who believe their team rarely follows through on initiatives will encounter any new initiative with suspicion. If the norms within the group don't support implementation of a system, any effort is doomed. I recall working with an organization to help the team become more effective and having a team member in response to a suggestion say, "Okay, when that doesn't work, what should I do?" This response told me that there were fundamental issues that needed to be addressed before we could reasonably move forward.

Not the least of these fundamental issues is the norm that I call "yahbutosis." It's fine, for example to raise questions about ideas, but if the autonomic response is "yah, but" you have yahbutosis and you need a yahbutectomy! Said another way, the team's or organization's culture in this instance must be addressed before you can move toward system implementation. In addition, in support of the earlier point, I suspect that the individual's supervision wasn't truly steeped in employee engagement and performance management practices and one might surmise that there is a dearth of strong leadership practice, as well. All of which is to say that each of the chapters build upon each other and are interdependent.

Most nonprofit organizations are involved in helping to better our society and the world around us. Whether it's the local YMCA, the Forest Preservation Society, or a child welfare service organization, nonprofits are working to change some part of the world for the better. Given that this is a driving force, Chapter 8 becomes an important frame for considering how to support change within the organization itself. As you read through the chapter you saw how I worked to provide you with a variety of conceptual lenses as well as specific strategies to ensure successful change management. Ideally, you will develop your organization's culture so that there is a propensity to be continually refining and developing your services, programs, systems, and capacity to realize the agency's mission. To build a culture that embraces continuous change is to arm yourself with a dynamic and responsive organization. I have watched organizations that have leveraged their ability to respond to the various forms of change become wildly successful, even in the face of dire situations, such as the COVID-19 pandemic. On the other hand, organizations that have a difficult time with change often are unable to pivot in time and have trouble being as flexible as they need to be. Pursuing the ideas explored in Chapter 8 will help you to ensure that your organization is in the *wildly successful* category.

As we think about the interconnectivity between the various frames, it is interesting to note how the ability to effectively manage conflict is intricately connected to many of the other frames. Change management, for example, often is a source of conflict for organizations. As you will recall, my friend always said he "doesn't mind change as long as it doesn't matter." When we try to help move a change initiative forward, there is often a point of conflict that ensues as people begin to feel that what is being asked of them truly matters to them. Knowing how to manage conflict and having the ability to implement and leverage some of the strategies we explore in Chapter 9 are part and parcel to you and your team's leadership successes.

Similarly, conflict management and how it is handled is closely tied to organizational culture. Building a strong organizational culture— one that is mission- and vision-focused with clearly articulated and acted-upon values and beliefs—is like having a strong immune system.

In this metaphor, the stronger your immune system, the better able you are to withstand the conflict that is inherent in the change process. You can build your immune system and hence your organization's ability to not only work through but also leverage conflict by implementing the various strategies discussed in Chapter 4.

In addition, Chapter 9 explores specific strategies to address conflict within the team and the organization. In the Appendix you will find an assessment tool related to conflict management strategies. The tool asks you to rate both your own ability to use a given strategy (on a scale of 1 to 5, with 1 meaning "needs help" and 5 meaning "awesome"), as well as your team's ability within each conflict management strategy. Once you have completed the rating, consider the activities that you will use to help you and your team as well as the overall agency be more effective at managing and optimizing the opportunities that conflict presents.

Of course, besides the strength of your team, your ability to help them reach their full potential serves as another critical framework for leadership and management success within nonprofit organizations. Making sure people have the training and tools that they need, ensuring that your own supervisory practice is strong, allowing for ownership on the part of your employees, and leveraging leadership behavior using effective feedback techniques become pivotal in assuring your team's success.

I have included another tool to help you think about your own supervisory practice. As we discussed in Chapter 10 it is critical that you have not only the self-awareness necessary to be a good supervisor but also the skills needed. Utilize the tool in the Appendix to help you gain awareness as well as develop some strategies to ensure that your supervisory practice is the best possible.

Working with your team is an important part of a framework for successful leadership practice and it is intricately connected to the other strategies we have explored. Being the best leader possible, having systems to support communication and teamwork—while using strategies for full-on employee engagement—are but a few of the points of intersection. I can tell you from my own experience that my success as a leader over these many years is largely because I have consistently had great team members who are willing and ultimately quite able to support the mission and vision of the organization. Do not forget the importance of the team in your and your organization's success. For this reason, work to optimize the recommendations and suggestions that I have included in Chapter 10, as well as recognize how inextricably interconnected team development is within the overall framework for leadership success.

In Chapter 11 we take a turn and focus on the external operating environment and the possibilities presented by various types of strategic alliances. It is important to recognize that there is an entire world operating outside the boundaries of your nonprofit organization. Being fully engaged in the external environment as well as being aware of the possibilities that strategic alliances in their various forms present is extremely important. We could dedicate an entire book to this aspect of our framework for success. Instead, I have provided you with some reference points about the types of alliance that are possible, as well as some of the challenges and opportunities that you might encounter.

As a brief primer I believe that Chapter 11 provides you with some important considerations when it comes to developing strategic alliances with external partners. I would also suggest that the first 10 chapters also provide you with a type of litmus test for any organization with which you might want to develop a more formal relationship. What does their employee engagement look like, for example? Do you see alignment between mission, vision, values, beliefs, and behaviors across the organization? What are the systems that are in place to help support the organization's operations, and do they meet the principles that we have explored? Questions like these can help you to utilize the strategies explored in the first 10 chapters to better understand how to explore more formal strategic alliances.

I hope that you have found the strategies for successful leadership shared throughout this book helpful. The various topics explored at the individual, team, and organizational level come together to provide you with a framework for efficacy as you work to develop your own leadership capacity. Together they represent an opportunity for you to advance your leadership and through this the ability for your nonprofit organization to achieve success. I recognize that there are many layers here and that your ability to realize impact is directly connected to the role that you have within the organization and the organizational context that is at hand. Even if you find yourself in a role that has limited capacity to provide impact, knowing how to ensure the success of the organization is essential. The leadership journey is not a static experience, but rather one that is dynamic, and it will only be a matter of time before you find a window open that enables you to implement one or more of the strategies we have talked about within the various chapters.

I share a metaphor with my students and employees that helps to describe how the many strategies we have explored come together to support a framework for successful leadership practice. Have you been to the symphony? A symphony is a collection of various instruments that come together to create a beautiful piece of music. Each section of the orchestra, each instrument, and each musician has a role to play. When they are aligned, in tune, and in step with the conductor, the sound is beautiful. Working to successfully implement the various strategies laid out in this book will help to ensure that your organization is able to create a beautiful sound. Through the strategies, you will develop your own leadership practice, in part by heightened mastery of your practice perspectives, and then through the engagement of specific strategies, and by your choice of leadership style.

Your efforts to create a positive organizational culture will yield benefits and the way you work to build generative leadership between and among your team members will yield positive results. These efforts, too, will benefit from the full engagement of your employees and the systems that you build, based on the practical examples and suggestions in this book that will help to raise up the team and support their ongoing success. The strategies explored to address change and conflict management will also help to ensure that the team you build is a strong one. And then, along the way, the ability to work strategically with the external environment through strategic alliances provides yet another opportunity to advance the success of your leadership practice and ultimately the success of the organization.

Just like an orchestra, there are many moving parts involved here. With practice, though, each part can and will come together to help assure success. Have you ever arrived early to the symphony and heard the tuning that is going on? The sound can be godawful. It is important to note that while it initially sounds pretty bad, the process of tuning the instruments is a necessary one, ensuring the beautiful sound that is to come. Similarly, there are elements of this overall framework for success that may sound unobtainable, at least to start with, but as you perfect the use of each strategy and fine-tune your efforts, you will see that success is not only possible but assured.

References

Allen, N. J., & Meyer, J. P. (1996). Affective, continuance, and normative commitment to the organization: An examination of construct validity. *Journal of Vocational Behavior, 49*(3), 252–276.

Allert, J. R., & Chatterjee, S. R. (1997). Corporate communication and trust in leadership. *Corporate Communications, 2*(1), 14–22.

Andrews, D., & Crowther, F. (2002). Parallel leadership: A clue to the contents of the "black box" of school reform. *The International Journal of Educational Management, 16*(4/5), 152–159.

Aryani, R., & Widodo, W. (2020). The determinant of organizational culture and its impact on organization: A conceptual framework. *International Journal of Higher Education, 9*(3), 64–70.

Argyris, C., Putnam, R., & McLain Smith, D. (1985). *Action science: Concepts, methods, and skills for research and intervention* (1st ed.). San Francisco, CA: Jossey-Bass.

Ayoobzadeh, M., & Boies, K. (2020). From mentors to leaders: Leader development outcomes for mentors. *Journal of Managerial Psychology, 35*(6), 497.

Baxter, L. A., & Montgomery, B. M. (1996). *Relating: Dialogues and dialectics.* New York: Guilford Press.

Bell, T. P. (2015). Meditative practice cultivates mindfulness and reduces anxiety, depression, blood pressure, and heart rate in a diverse sample. *Journal of Cognitive Psychotherapy, 29*(4), 343–355. https://doi.org.nec.gmilcs.org/10.1891/0889-8391.29.4.343

Bennet, A., & Bennet, D. (2004). *Organizational survival in the new world: The intelligent complex adaptive system.* Amsterdam: Elsevier Butterworth-Heinemann.

Bennis, W., Goleman, D., O'Toole, J., & Ward Biderman, P. (2008). *Transparency: How leaders create a culture of candor* (1st ed.). San Francisco, CA: Jossey-Bass.

Blanchard, K., & Broadwell, R. (2018). *Servant leadership in action: How you can achieve great relationships and results.* San Francisco, CA: Berrett-Koehler.

Blumer, H. (1969). *Symbolic interactionism: Perspective and method.* Englewood Cliffs, NJ: Prentice-Hall.

Burke, S. C., Sims, D. E., Lazzara, E. H., & Salas, E. (2007). Trust in leadership: A multi-level review and integration. *The Leadership Quarterly, 18*(6), 606–632.

Cangemi, J., & Miller, R. (2007). Breaking out of the box in organizations: Structuring a positive climate for the development of creativity in the workplace. *Journal of Management Development, 26*(5), 401–410.

Carpenter, J., Webb, C., & Bostock, L. (2013). The surprisingly weak evidence base for supervision: Findings from a systematic review of research in child welfare practice (2000–2012). *Children and Youth Services Review, 35*(11), 1843–1853.

Chin, B., Lindsay, E. K., Greco, C. M., Brown, K. W., Smyth, J. M., Wright, A. G. C., & Creswell, J. D. (2019). Psychological mechanisms driving stress resilience in mindfulness training: A randomized controlled trial. *Health Psychology: Official Journal of the Division of Health Psychology, American Psychological Association, 38*(8), 759–768. https://doi-org.nec.gmilcs.org/10.1037/hea0000763

Clardy, A. (2018). Managing organizational conflict: Towards a comprehensive framework of outcomes, practices, and competencies. *Performance Improvement, 57*(10), 10–25. https://doi-org.nec.gmilcs.org/10.1002/pfi.21810

Collins, J. C. (2001). *Good to great: Why some companies make the leap . . . and others don't.* New York: HarperCollins.

Creating a culture of innovation. (2013). *Development and Learning in Organizations, 27*(2), 26–29.

Dann, P. (2008). *Emergent leadership models and generative leadership: Research toward new leadership paradigms in nonprofit organizations.* Unpublished doctoral dissertation, Fielding Graduate University, Santa Barbara, CA.

Deal, T. E., & Kennedy, A. A. (1982). *Corporate cultures: The rites and rituals of corporate life.* Harmondsworth: Penguin Books; reissue Perseus Books, 2000.

Doh, J. P. (2003). Can leadership be taught? Perspectives from management educators. *Academy of Management Learning and Education, 2*(1), 54–67. https://doi.org/10.5465/AMLE.2003.9324025

Drucker, P. (2006). *The effective executive: The definitive guide to getting the right things done*. New York: Harper Business.

Erikson, E. H. (1993). *Childhood and society*. New York: W. W. Norton and Company.

Feldman, D. C. (1984). The development and enforcement of group norms. *Academy of Management Review, 9*(1), 47–53. https://doi.org/10.5465/AMR.1984.4277934

Frost, D. E., Fiedler, F. E., & Anderson, J. W. (1983). The role of personal risk-taking in effective leadership. *Human Relations, 36*(2), 185–202.

Gelfand, M. J., Leslie, L. M., Keller, K., & de Dreu, C. (2012). Conflict cultures in organizations: How leaders shape conflict cultures and their organizational-level consequences. *Journal of Applied Psychology, 97*(6), 1131–1147. https://doi-org.nec.gmilcs.org/10.1037/a0029993

Gladwell, M. (2008). *Outliers: The story of success*. New York: Little, Brown and Co., 2008.

Greenleaf, Robert. (1977). *Servant leadership: A journey into the nature of legitimate power and greatness*. New York: Paulist Press.

Johnson, G., & Leavitt, W. (2001). Building on success: Transforming organizations through an appreciative inquiry. *Public Personnel Management, 30*(1), 129. https://doi.org/10.1177/009102600103000111

Johnson, W. B., & Smith, D. G. (2019, December 30). Real mentorship starts with company culture, not formal programs. *Harvard Business Review Digital Articles*, 2–5.

Kluger, J. (2008) *Simplexity: Why simple things become complex (and how complex things can be made simple)*. New York: Hyperion.

Knoster, T., Villa, T., & Thousand, J., (2000). A framework for thinking about systems change. In R. Villa & J. Thousand (Eds.), *Restructuring for caring and effective education: Piecing the puzzle together* (pp. 93–128). Baltimore, MD: Paul H. Brookes.

Koestler, Arthur (1967). *The ghost in the machine* (1990 reprint ed.). Penguin Group.

Kotter, J. (1996). *Leading change*. Cambridge, MA: Harvard Business School Press.

Lawrence, H. V., & Wiswell, A. K. (1993). Using the workgroup as a laboratory for learning: Increasing leadership and team effectiveness through feedback. *Human Resource Development Quarterly, 4*(2), 135–149.

Lencioni, P. (2013). The advantage. *Leadership Excellence, 30*(4), 16–17.

Lee, P., Gillespie, N., Mann, L., & Wearing, A. (2010). Leadership and trust: Their effect on knowledge sharing and team performance. *Management*

Learning. 41(4), 473–491. Accessed June 19, 2021. https://search-ebscohost-com.nec.gmilcs.org/login.aspx?direct=trueanddb=edbandAN=53291091ands ite=eds-liveandscope=site

Lewin, K. (1948). Frontiers of group dynamics. *Human Relations, 1,* 5–41.

Lewin, K. (1951). *Field theory in social science: Selected theoretical papers* (1st ed.). New York: Harper.

Luft, J., & Ingham, H. (1955). The Johari window, a graphic model of interpersonal awareness. *Proceedings of the Western Training Laboratory in Group Development.* Los Angeles, CA: UCLA.

Marcos, A., García-Ael, C., & Topa, G. (2020). The influence of work resources, demands, and organizational culture on job satisfaction, organizational commitment, and citizenship behaviors of Spanish police officers. *International Journal of Environmental Research and Public Health, 17*(20). https://doi .org/10.3390/ijerph17207607

Marion, R., & Uhl-Bien, M. (2001). Leadership in complex organizations. *Leadership Quarterly, 12*(4), 389. https://doi-org.nec.gmilcs.org/10.1016/S1048-9843(01)00092-3

McEvily, B., Perrone, V., & Zaheer, A. (2003). Trust as an organizing principle. *Organizational Science, 14*(1), 91–103.

Morden, T. (1997). Leadership as vision. *Management Decision, 35*(9).

Mone, E. M., & London, M. (2009). *Employee engagement through effective performance management: A practical guide for managers.* New York: Routledge.

Mone, E., Eisinger, C., Guggenheim, K., Price, B., & Stine, C. (2011). Performance management at the wheel: Driving employee engagement in organizations. *Journal of Business and Psychology, 26*(2), 205–212.

Morgan, G. (1996). *Images of organization.* New International Edition. Thousand Oaks, CA: Sage.

Morrison, T. (2005). *Staff supervision in social care: Making a real difference for staff and service users* (Rev. ed.). Brighton, UK: Pavilion.

Nadler, D. A., & Tushman, M. L. (1990). Beyond the charismatic leader: Leadership and organizational change. *California Management Review, 32*(2), 77–97.

Neilson, G., Martin, K., & Powers, E. (2008). The secrets to successful strategy execution. *Harvard Business Review, 86*(6), 60–70, 138.

O'Toole, J. (1996). *Leading change: Overcoming the ideology of comfort and the tyranny of custom.* New York: Wiley.

Pascale, R. T. (1999, April 15). Surfing the edge of chaos. *Sloan Management Review,* 83–94.

Pearce, C. L., & Conger, J. A. (Eds.) (2003). *Shared leadership.* Thousand Oaks, CA: Sage.

Phipps, S. T. A., Prieto, L. C., & Ndinguri, E. N. (2013). Understanding the impact of employee involvement on organizational productivity: The moderating role of organizational commitment. *Journal of Organizational Culture, Communication and Conflict, 17*(2), 107–120.

Probert, J., & Turnbull James, K. (2011). Leadership development: Crisis, opportunities and the leadership concept. *Leadership, 7*(2), 137–150.

Radulovic, A. B., Thomas, G., Epitropaki, O., & Legood, A. (2019). Forgiveness in leader–member exchange relationships: Mediating and moderating mechanisms. *Journal of Occupational and Organizational Psychology, 92*(3), 498–534. https://doi-org.nec.gmilcs.org/10.1111/joop.12274

Raelin, J. (2003). *Creating leaderful organizations: How to bring out the leadership in everyone* (1st ed.). San Francisco, CA: Berrett-Koehler.

Raelin, J. (2011). From leadership-as-practice to leaderful practice. *Leadership, 7*(2), 195–211.

Rost, J. C. (1993). *Leadership for the twenty-first century*. Westport, CT: Praeger.

Rotchford, N. (2002). Performance management. In J.W. Hedge & E. D. Pulakos (Eds.), *Implementing organizational interventions* (pp. 167–197). San Francisco, CA: Jossey-Bass.

Rozovsky, J. (2015). *The five keys to a successful Google team*. Google People Operations.

Schachter, S., & Gazzaniga, M. (Eds.). (1990). A theory of cognitive dissonance. In *Extending psychological frontiers: Selected works of Leon Festinger* (pp. 201–237). New York: Russell Sage Foundation.

Schein, E. (2002). The anxiety of learning. Interview by Diane L. Coutu. *Harvard Business Review, 80*(3), 100.

Schmidt, S., & Eisend, M. (2015). Advertising repetition: A meta-analysis on effective frequency in advertising. *Journal of Advertising, 44*(4), 415–428. https://doi.org/10.1080/00913367.2015.1018460

Seers, A. (2004). *Leadership and flexible organizational structures*. Greenwich, CT: Information Age.

Smither, J. W., London, M., & Reilly, R. R. (2005). Does performance improve following multisource feedback? A theoretical model, meta-analysis, and review of empirical findings. *Personnel Psychology, 58*, 33–66.

Spillane, J. P. (2006). *Distributed leadership*. San Francisco, CA: Jossey-Bass.

Strebel, J. (1998). *Harvard Business Review on change*. Boston: Harvard Business School Publishing.

Tannenbaum, R., & Schmidt, W. H. (1973). How to choose a leadership pattern. *Harvard Business Review, 51*(3), 162–180.

Thomas, R. J. (2008). Life's hard lessons. *HR Magazine, 53*(6), 143–146.

Tohme, O., & Joseph, S. (2020). Authenticity is correlated with mindfulness and emotional intelligence. *Journal of Humanistic Psychology, 1*. https://doi-org .nec.gmilcs.org/10.1177/0022167820940926

Tomlinson, J. (2007). *The culture of speed: The coming of immediacy*. Thousand Oaks, CA, & London: Sage, 2007.

Torbert, W. R., & Cook-Greuter, S. R. (2004). *Action inquiry: The secret of timely and transforming leadership*. San Francisco, CA: Berrett-Koehler.

Tropman, J., & Blackburn, J. A. (2018). The necessary traits of exemplary leadership. *Effective Executive, 21*(3), 7–13.

Virgana, V., & Kasyadi, S. (2020). The effect of organizational culture, personality, job satisfaction, and trust on school supervisor performance. *Journal of Education and Learning (EduLearn), 14*(3), 434–441.

Wasylkiw, L., Holton, J., Azar, R., and Cook, W. (2015). The impact of mindfulness on leadership effectiveness in a health care setting: A pilot study. *Journal of Health Organization and Management, 29*(7), 893–911. https://doi-org.nec .gmilcs.org/10.1108/JHOM-06-2014-0099

Wilber, K. (1996). *A brief history of everything* (1st ed.). Boston: Shambhala.

Weiner, B. (2009). A theory of organizational readiness for change. *Implementation Science, 19*(4), 67.

Weigold, M., & Schlenker, B. R. (1991). Accountability and risk-taking. *Society for Personality and Social Psychology, 17*(1), 25–29.

Wolf, E., & Zwick, T. (2008). Reassessing the productivity impact of employee involvement and financial incentives. *Schmalenbach Business Review (SBR), 60*(2), 160–181.

Wonnacott, J. (2014). *Developing and supporting effective staff supervision: A reader to support the delivery of staff supervision training for those working with vulnerable children, adults and their families*. Hove, UK: Pavilion. Retrieved from http:// www.ebrary.com

Woten, M. R. B., and Mennella, H. D. A.-B. (2018). Conflict management (The Joint Commission, 2018). *CINAHL Nursing Guide* (Ipswich, MA: EBSCO).

Appendix: Tools to Help Build Leadership Practice

Mindfulness Exercises

Mindfulness exercises help you develop your ability to be aware. The literature, for example, shows that individuals who practice mindfulness have less stress in their lives, are better able to focus on tasks that are at hand, and are perceived to be genuine and authentic by those around them (Wasylkiw, Azar, & Cook, 2015). All of this helps to advance one's leadership practice and ability to be effective as a leader. The following exercises are quite simple and take only a few minutes of your time each day.

Mindful Breathing

This is my favorite mindfulness exercise and can be done anywhere. The trick is to start by breathing in slowly through your nose and then exhaling through your mouth. As you do this, close your eyes and focus on the sensation that you experience as you bring in a new breath of fresh air and then exhale. Do this for a few minutes each day and you will immediately find a positive effect. Your mind will settle down and, as noted above, you will reap the benefits of mindfulness practice.

Mindful Observation

Find a time and space to simply observe what is going on around you. As an example, I have a grand old oak tree that I walk under and simply look up to observe the leaves and the branches above me. I allow my focus to be solely on the tree, its color, the way the wind moves the branches, and absorbing the overall experience of settling my mind to simply observe. This exercise will provide you with benefits associated with mindfulness practice. Another strategy I use for this is to change my view when walking by, looking up instead of looking down. This is quite remarkable and you'll find that just a five-minute walk using this technique will help reduce stress and ground you more to the task at hand.

Mindful Awareness

In this exercise you sit still and raise your awareness about all that is happening around you. What sounds do you hear, who is around you, what is the physical environment that surrounds you? Take time to heighten your awareness about all that's going on around you. Be present and in the moment as you become mindfully aware of your surroundings. You will be quite surprised to see how this exercise helps you to slow down and be calmer as well as more focused.

Mindful Listening

Like the mindful awareness exercise, this exercise asks you to become more aware, but from an auditory standpoint. Find a spot to sit quietly and then simply focus on what you hear. How many sounds surround you? Are you surprised to realize that there are multiple sounds that you now hear? Focus solely on the sounds, allowing your brain to filter out all the pressures and demands that the day has presented. This exercise will also provide the benefits associated with mindfulness practice and can be done anywhere!

Mindful Appreciation

Mindful appreciation is another one of my favorite mindfulness exercises. In this exercise you can simply take a few minutes to consider all the things that you are appreciative of. What are you thankful for? Build a list in your mind of all that you have to be appreciative of. Sit quietly for a few minutes to allow yourself to truly consider why you are thankful. Consider the elements of each item on your mental list and take a moment to relish the positive nature of what you appreciate. We know from the literature that thinking about things you appreciate helps you to feel more positive, which helps to manage stress, making it easier to focus on the task at hand.

Leadership Practice Perspective Assessment Tool

Use this assessment tool to rate your abilities within each of the eight practice perspectives discussed in Chapter 2. Once you have rated yourself, take a moment to reflect on each practice perspective and then consider strategies that you can use to build your capability in each area.

Practice Perspective	Related Attributes	1–10 Score (1 equals plenty of room to grow and 10 means "You've got this!")	Strategies
Being Antigravitational	I know when the best course of action is against the flow.		
The Long View	I am tenacious. I can be patient and know when to act or stand back.		
It's the Journey, Not the Destination	I am able to enjoy the journey. I am able to be present. I see how the journey can inform the end goal.		

Practice Perspective	Related Attributes	1–10 Score (1 equals plenty of room to grow and 10 means "You've got this!")	Strategies
Use a Compass, Not a Road Map	I am flexible and can adapt. I understand how to pivot.		
Leverage Serendipity	I am prepared to make use of surprises. I am ready for opportunity to present itself.		
Awareness	I regularly strive to develop my own self-awareness.		
Address Inner Pressures	I am aware of internal dialogue. I can adapt my approach to manage my self-talk.		
Hero Leader versus Leading Heroes	I give credit to my team. I work to build leaders on my team.		

Servant Leadership Assessment Tool

Read Chapter 3 and the 10 key characteristics of servant leadership, then rate yourself and consider areas for your own growth. Use this assessment tool with colleagues to prompt discussion of shared strategies for growth.

Servant Leadership Characteristics	Attributes	1–10 Score (1 equals plenty of room to grow and 10 means "You've got this!")	Strategies
Listening	■ Desire to understand ■ Listening to what is *not* said		
Empathy	■ Seek to understand each individual as a person		
Healing	■ Help others solve problems and resolve conflicts ■ Build a culture free of fear		
Awareness	■ Of self ■ Being integrated and holistic		
Persuasion	■ Active engagement to convince		

Servant Leadership Characteristics	Attributes	1–10 Score (1 equals plenty of room to grow and 10 means "You've got this!")	Strategies
Conceptualization	■ Seeing beyond the day-to-day activities ■ Having a personal and professional vision		
Foresight	■ Capacity to anticipate outcomes ■ Capacity to anticipate consequences		
Stewardship	■ Holding the organization in trust for the betterment of society ■ Belief in an obligation to serve		
Commitment to Growth	■ Encouraging personal, professional, and spiritual growth		
Commitment to Building Strong Community	■ Within the organization and within the larger community		
Total Score			

Generative Leadership® Questionnaire

Building generative leadership capacity across your team and the agency will improve leadership practice for the entire organization. Please complete the following questionnaire, rating each question by using the scale provided. Once you have completed the questionnaire, total your scores for each core element and subtheme on the attached scoring sheet. (Note: Team = Your most immediate work group; Organization = The agency.)

Date:

Name (Optional):   Position:

Organization/Program:

Theme	SELF-RATING				
	Strongly Agree (5)	Agree (4)	Somewhat Agree (3)	Disagree (2)	Strongly Disagree (1)	Don't Know (0)
Opportunity					
1. I have the opportunity to take on leadership responsibility.					
2. I can think of opportunities for team members to take on leadership roles within the team.					

3. The organization provides opportunities to take on leadership responsibilities.					
Risk-Taking					
4. I'm willing to take a risk and assume leadership responsibilities.					
5. I regularly see other team members willing to take on leadership responsibility.					
6. The organization encourages me to step outside of my comfort zone.					
Trust					
7. I trust my supervisor.					
8. There is a strong sense of trust among my team members.					
9. I believe that the organization trusts its employees.					
Individual Leadership Attributes					
10. I feel competent in my personal leadership ability.					

(continued)

Theme	SELF-RATING					
	Strongly Agree (5)	Agree (4)	Somewhat Agree (3)	Disagree (2)	Strongly Disagree (1)	Don't Know (0)
Individual Leadership Attributes (*continued*)						
11. My team members have strong leadership capabilities.						
12. I feel confident in the organization's leaders.						
Communication and Feedback						
13. My communication and feedback skills are strong.						
14. We have a high level of communication and feedback within our team.						
15. I feel there is a high level of communication and feedback at an organizational level.						
Expectations						
16. My supervisor expects me to engage in leadership behavior.						
17. The team expects each member to take on leadership behavior.						

18. The organization expects each of us to be leaders in our own right.				
Having a Voice				
19. I feel heard.				
20. The team members value each other's input.				
21. Employee input matters to the organization.				
Commitment				
22. I feel committed to my work.				
23. The team is committed to the work.				
24. The organization is committed to this work.				
Perceived Need to Act				
25. I often feel the need to take on leadership responsibility.				
26. The team knows when it is time to take on leadership responsibilities.				
27. I feel that the leadership at the organizational level knows when it is time to act by taking on leadership behavior.				

(continued)

Theme	SELF-RATING					
	Strongly Agree (5)	Agree (4)	Somewhat Agree (3)	Disagree (2)	Strongly Disagree (1)	Don't Know (0)
Organizational Practice and Philosophy						
28. The organization believes that I should exercise leadership behavior.						
29. I feel the organization supports the team to be leaders.						
30. The organization believes that we should all take on leadership behavior.						
Role Modeling						
31. I role model leadership behavior.						
32. The team role models leadership behavior.						
33. I believe that leaders at the organizational level role model leadership behavior.						

Shared Beliefs and Values							
34. I share the values and beliefs of the team.							
35. The team shares the values and beliefs of the organization.							
36. Shared values and beliefs are present throughout the organization.							
Structure							
37. The systems we use help to support my leadership behavior.							
38. The systems we use support leadership behavior within the team.							
39. The systems used at the organizational level promote leadership behavior.							

Generative Leadership Questionnaire Scoring Sheet

Generative Leadership Questionnaire	Category Score	
Core Element		**Comments and Action Steps**
Opportunity		
Risk-Taking		
Trust		
Individual Leadership Attributes		
Communication and Feedback		
Expectations		
Core Element Rating Total		
Subtheme	**Category Score**	
Having a Voice		
Commitment		
Perceived Need to Act		
Organizational Philosophy and Practice		
Role Modeling		
Shared Beliefs and Values		
Structure		
Subtheme Rating Total		

Score Interpretation

Each category represents a theme that supports the co-creation of leadership within leadership teams. The highest possible score for each individual theme is 15, with the possible score for the core elements totaling 90, subthemes totaling 105, and a potential combined score of 195.

Use the attached score sheet to pull together your scores by core element and subtheme, as well as in total. Once you have done this, proceed to the suggestions below.

One strategy is to look at the themes individually and consider what actions might be taken to support generative leadership within the given theme. For example, if the scores are low at the team level for role modeling, then an action step might be to talk about the importance of role modeling with the team while identifying specific behaviors to role model as well as behaviors to eliminate because they do not support effective leadership.

Below is a breakdown for interpreting the combined score of all 13 themes:

175–195	Excellent Generative Leadership Capacity
156–175	Very Strong Generative Leadership Capacity
136–156	Strong Generative Leadership Capacity
117–136	Generative Leadership Potential Is Present
97–117	There's Work to Be Done!
78–97	"Heavy Lifting" Needed Here
0–78	Uh-ohh!!

The questions within each theme are also designed to explore the presence of generative leadership at the individual, team, and organizational levels. Therefore, analysis can be conducted by looking at the total generative leadership capability at each separate level (the individual, team, and organizational levels). To conduct this analysis for the individual level, total the first question for each theme; for the team level, total the second question for each theme; and for the organizational level, total the third question for each theme. The worksheet below is designed to make this easier.

Generative Leadership Capacity at the Three Levels

Question Number	Score	Question Number	Score	Question Number	Score
1.		2.		3.	
4.		5.		6.	
7.		8.		9.	
10.		11.		12.	
13.		14.		15.	
16.		17.		18.	
19.		20.		21.	
22.		23.		24.	
25.		26.		27.	
28.		29.		30.	
31.		32.		33.	
34.		35.		36.	
37.		38.		39.	
Total Score—Individual Level		Total Score—Team Level		Total Score—Organizational Level	

Below is a breakdown for interpreting your score at the three individual levels.

60–65	Excellent Generative Leadership Capacity
50–59	Very Strong Generative Leadership Capacity
42–51	Strong Generative Leadership Capacity
32–41	Generative Leadership Potential Is Present
22–31	There's Work to Be Done!
10–21	"Heavy lifting" Here
0–9	"Uh-ohh!!"

Source: Paul L. Dann, PhD. © Copyright 2009.

Through this analysis, it becomes possible to target your action steps toward a specific level. It might be, for example, that the team level scores low, so strategies should be tailored to support the development of the team.

The Generative Leadership Questionnaire can be used by the individual, the team, or the entire organization to consider the nature of leadership that is present and the ability to co-create leadership.

Performance Management Assessment

This tool is designed for supervisors to rate their behavior for providing performance management activities with their employees. The assessment makes it possible for the supervisor to rate their performance management behavior with up to six subordinates. The tool can also be used by employees to rate their supervisor. To use the assessment, rate each topic area using a 1-to-5 scale with a score of 1 equaling "never" and a score of 5 equaling "always."

Performance Management Activity	Manager Behaviors for Effective Performance Management	Team Member 1	Team Member 2	Team Member 3	Team Member 4	Team Member 5	Team Member 6	Comments
Setting performance and development goals	Jointly setting goals Helping employees understand how their work supports the overall company strategy and direction							
Providing ongoing feedback and recognition	Providing a satisfactory amount of recognition							

	Providing feedback that helps improve performance			
Managing employee development	Providing sufficient opportunities for training			
	Supporting career development efforts			
	Conducting career-planning discussions			
Conducting mid-year and year-end appraisals	Conducting an effective performance appraisal discussion			
Building a climate of trust and empowerment with employees	Encouragement to be innovative and creative			
	Encouragement to improve work processes and productivity			
	Valuing ideas and opinions			

System Assessment Tool

This tool can help you determine whether the systems you use are aligned with key principles for success. As we discussed in Chapter 7 the implementation and use of well-laid-out systems will leverage your leadership capacity as well as your organization's ability to realize its mission and vision.

Specific System _____			
System Principle	Key Thoughts	Score	Comment
Mission Centered	All systems should support the organization's mission.		
Aligned with the Vision	Be sure your vision is clearly articulated, and that each system supports the agency's vision.		
Support the Values and Beliefs	Systems that are misaligned with the agency's values and beliefs will harm the organization's ability to achieve the desired mission.		
Maintaining Both Efficacy and Efficiency	It's essential to manage the upside of each polarity. Be careful not to pursue efficiency at the cost of efficacy.		
Building the "We"	Building mission- and vision-centered belonging helps you get to yes (*oui!*). Be sure your systems support this outcome.		
Meaning Making	We use internal as well as social practices to develop meaning. Meaning translates into what we believe and belief drives behavior. Work to ensure that systems create synergy of meaning to help drive effective behavior.		

Use this assessment tool to determine your and your team's areas of strength and areas for growth when it comes to the conflict management strategies explored in Chapter 9. Rate yourself and your team, then consider ways in which you can improve the organization's capacity to leverage conflict for better agency outcomes. Also have your team members complete the assessment. How do your scores compare? Do you agree? How might you join forces to enhance your team's capability in this important area?

Conflict Management Strategies Tool

	Key Elements	Your Score (1–5)	Team's Score (1–5)	Comments and Strategies to Improve
Proactive Engagement	Stay ahead of conflict by ensuring that challenges and issues are addressed early on.			
Communication	Practice direct and intentional communication to ensure that loops are closed and feedback is provided directly to those involved. Support dialectical as well as dialogical communication. Work to break down assumptions and provide clear understanding about differing perspectives.			

(continued)

	Key Elements	Your Score (1–5)	Team's Score (1–5)	Comments and Strategies to Improve
Mission Focused	Stick to the mission. Ensure that conflict resolution helps to support mission-focused behavior.			
Leadership Skills	Build on your practice perspectives. Work to develop trust and genuineness. Know when to tell, sell, consult, and join. Practice loose-tight controls.			
Operationalize Conflict	Include expectations that conflict will happen, and that it will be resolved, resulting in compromise and commitment for a path forward.			
Boundary Function of Leadership	Help define roles and responsibilities. Make sure to set standards for boundaries so that team members can pursue the work.			
Build Collaborative Culture	Develop norms that support problem-solving and teamwork toward mission-based solutions during times of conflict (and throughout day-to-day work activities).			

	Key Elements	Your Score (1–5)	Team's Score (1–5)	Comments and Strategies to Improve
Values and Beliefs Focused	Build strong values and beliefs within your organization's operations that can be drawn upon to support conflict resolution. Operationalize values such as respect, caring, and responsibility.			
Conflict as Opportunity	Conflict can serve as an opportunity to learn and grow, to consider alternative ways of doing things. Avoid tamping down and smoothing out conflict. Choose instead to lean into conflict and explore the presenting situation as an opportunity for learning and growth.			
Vision Work	Connect conflict resolution to the organization's vision. Ensure that solutions are aligned with the agency's vision.			

Johari Window Team Assessment Tool

Use this assessment tool to help you build awareness about your team's ability to work together. As we explored in Chapter 10 the goal is to build upon your and your team's ability to operate in the Open area of the Johari window. Answer the questions and then build strategies together to enhance the Open quadrant and reduce the Blind, the Unknown, and the Hidden quadrants for a more effective team. There are 15 possible Yes answers. The more you can honestly answer yes, the stronger your team is in its ability to work effectively together.

Blind Quadrant	Yes or No	Comments
1. Are we able to give each other feedback about work-related efforts?		
2. Am I open to receiving feedback from my team members?		
3. Do I ask for feedback from my team members so that I can be a better team member?		
4. Am I willing to hear something from a colleague that is uncomfortable?		
5. What are three strategies that we can work on together to help enhance our ability to give feedback?	Three Strategies	
Unknown Quadrant	Yes or No	Comments
1. Am I willing to try on new tasks and/or responsibilities?		
2. Does our team provide opportunities for members to try on new tasks or responsibilities?		

Unknown Quadrant (*continued*)	Yes or No	Comments
3. When a team member tries on a new responsibility are they provided with the training needed?		
4. As a team are we willing to risk taking on new responsibilities?		
5. Do we recognize team members for the skills that they are developing that were heretofore unknown to us?		
Hidden Quadrant	**Yes or No**	**Comments**
1. Do I feel safe to share my weaknesses with my supervisor?		
2. Do we communicate openly as a team or are there team members who are holding back?		
3. Do we regularly talk about each team member's areas for growth?		
4. Do we talk about the team's strengths and areas for growth?		
Open Quadrant	**Yes or No**	**Comments**
1. Does the team have a clear understanding of each team member's strengths and weaknesses?		
2. Are we regularly discussing strategies to build the Open quadrant?		
3. What are three strategies we can use to continue to expand the Open quadrant?	**Three Strategies**	

About the Author

PAUL L. DANN, PhD is a nationally recognized trainer and presenter in leadership, organizational development, and organizational culture. He serves as the executive director of NFI North, a multiservice behavioral health organization, and provides consultation for nonprofit organizations. He also teaches at the University of New Hampshire in the Carsey School of Public Policy.

He lives in New Hampshire with his wife.

Index